More Incredible Answers to Prayer

More Incredible Answers to Prayer

Roger J. Morneau

Review and Herald® Publishing Association
Hagerstown, MD 21740

The author assumes full responsibility for the accuracy of all facts and quotations as cited in this book.

This book was
Edited by Gerald Wheeler
Designed by Bill Kirstein
Cover design by Lee Cherry
Cover photo by Robin Smith/Tony Stone Worldwide
Typeset: 11/12.5 Novarese Medium

PRINTED IN U.S.A.

02 01 00 11 10 9

R&H Cataloging Service
Morneau, Roger J. 1925-1998
More incredible answers to prayer.

1. Prayer. 2. Warfare, Spiritual. 3. Spiritualism. I. Title.

248.3

ISBN 0-8280-0719-5

Dedication

This book is dedicated to the hundreds of readers who have encouraged me to share with others the continued answers to my prayers.

I have changed most of the names in this book to protect their privacy.

Preface

More than two years have passed since *Incredible Answers to Prayer* came off the press. During that time I have received hundreds of letters and phone calls. Some were prayer requests from people in need, but a large number were from people who wanted to tell me how the Lord had been blessing them as they interceded for others.

The Spirit of God has been transforming lives, remedying desperate conditions, and providing victory for the hopeless. In this new book I am presenting some of those marvelous stories. In addition, certain questions kept appearing over and over in those letters and telephone calls. They centered on demon possession and so-called deliverance ministries. I want to present in a more permanent form what I shared with those troubled individuals.

Roger J. Morneau

I Am a Specialist

I am a door opener. My specialty
consists of opening doors that have
been shut tight.
Some have been sealed shut and
boarded over.
Some have been bricked up.
Some have been secured with steel bars
and the walkway to them mined and barricaded.
All that effort has been put forth
by the enemies of righteousness to
assure themselves that their captives
will never experience freedom in Christ.
I am a specialist.
I am a door opener.
I am a praying man.

—Roger J. Morneau

Contents

CHAPTER

1

A Flood of Healing Grace

It is a medical miracle that I am alive today.

My most recent brush with death began one Saturday night as I prepared to retire for the evening about 10:30 p.m. Going to the bathroom, I suddenly found myself passing blood. Instantly I called my wife, Hilda. Although surprised at the sight of all that blood, she is a nurse and managed to remain calm. Opening a closet door, she grabbed a disposable diaper from a box that we kept on hand for our little granddaughter. Then she rushed me to the emergency room of one of the three hospitals of the Triple Cities area of southern New York.

Because I am on a blood thinner as a result of a heart condition, the emergency room physician was not able to stop the bleeding until 2:00 a.m. Sunday morning. Then I had to wait until the results from my lab work came back.

An orderly escorted me back from the lab to a small room. Pointing to a high, wheeled table, he said, "Please wait here, and the doctor will be with you shortly." About 15 minutes later the orderly returned and found me still standing there. "Oh! Mr. Morneau, you should be sitting down. Please wait, and I'll be right back." Seconds later he brought a footstool about 10 inches in height, placed it by my feet, and hurried out.

"That's an awfully small thing to sit on," I said to myself, "but it beats standing up." Making myself as comfortable on it as possible, I sat with my back against the frame of the table and my feet stretched out horizontally. Another 15 minutes passed. Then a nurse appeared holding a syringe with a long needle. "Hi! How are you doing down there?" she said, looking at me. "Sir, you should have used the footstool to step up and sit on the table."

Realizing how foolish I must have looked, I burst out laughing. The nurse gave me the injection, then departed with a smile, probably unable to wait to tell her colleagues about her befuddled patient.

A week later I received a phone call from a specialist in urology named Dr. Wise. He had gone over my test results and asked me to see him in his office the next day.

When I arrived at his office, he told me with the utmost tact and concern that I had cancer of the prostate. A large tumor had been the cause of my great loss of blood. The cancer had progressed beyond the point where it could be treated with chemotherapy. The only option left was surgery. After discussing my heart condition, he said he would consult with Dr. Smart, my cardiologist, about the risks of me undergoing surgery.

As I have mentioned in my previous book (*Incredible Answers to Prayer*), I had almost died in the intensive care unit of the Greater Niagara General Hospital back in December of 1984. Tests later revealed that a virus had destroyed a large part of my heart, leaving me disabled with cardiomyopathy, a disease of the heart muscle. Dr. Smart told my wife that he did not expect me to live longer than a few months, a fact that I did not learn until about a year ago.

In such cases the heart usually disintegrates until it kills the patient. In my case the heart tissue instead turned into a hard substance that I can compare only to leather. But with 60 percent of my heart destroyed and my blood constantly thinned to prevent clotting, I was a very poor candidate for any kind of surgery.

About 9:00 that evening the phone rang. To my surprise, it was Dr. Smart. He told me that he had spoken to the urologist about my having surgery and wanted to make sure that I understood the great risk I would be taking with my heart in such a weak condition. In fact, he believed that it was possible that I might not make it through the operation.

Hilda and I had a long conversation about what we should do; then we prayed for God to help us make an intelligent decision. That night I didn't sleep much as I considered my possible death. Yet as I looked back over my life I felt comforted by how the Lord had repeatedly intervened through the years.

Constantly God had wiped away tears, soothed pain, removed anxiety, dispelled fear, supplied wants, and bestowed unending blessings As I thought about what He had already done in my life, my faith strengthened, and I asked myself, "Why am I thinking about dying when I serve the living God, the Lord of Glory in whom dwelled 'the Spirit of life' [Romans 8:2]?"

Verses of Scripture began to fill my mind. "Like as a father pitieth his children, so the Lord pitieth them that fear him. For he knoweth our frame; he remembereth that we are dust" (Psalm 103:13, 14). "By him were all things created, that are in heaven, and that are in earth, visible and invisible, whether they be thrones, or dominions, or principalities, or powers: all things were created by him, and for him. And he is before all things, and by him all things consist" (Colossians 1:16, 17). "For in him dwelleth all the fullness of the Godhead bodily. And ye are complete in him, which is the head of all principality and power" (Colossians 2:9, 10).

Then my heart thrilled with a joy born of heaven as I considered Matthew 4:23, 24: "And Jesus went about all Galilee, teaching in their synagogues, and preaching the gospel of the kingdom, and healing all manner of sickness and all manner of disease among the people. And his fame went throughout all Syria: and they brought unto him all sick people that were taken with divers diseases and torments, and those which were possessed with devils, and those which were lunatick, and those that had the palsy; and he healed them."

And to top it all, a quotation from *The Desire of Ages* brought additional encouragement: "When the fullness of the time had come, the Deity was glorified by pouring upon the world a flood of healing grace that was never to be obstructed or withdrawn till the plan of salvation should be fulfilled" (p. 37). I understood *The Desire of Ages* to be teaching that God's healing grace was still available to each and every person who asked for it.

Encouraged and comforted, I began to pray.

"Precious Jesus, You are my strength and my Redeemer. As I look to the Holy of Holies of the heavenly sanctuary where You are ministering in behalf of fallen humanity, I thank You for leaving the courts of glory to come to this land of the enemy. Your blood, shed on the cross, has washed away all my iniquities and my sins, the errors of my ways and the evil of my fallen human heart. And for all the mercies of Thy love, and the blessings of Thy grace, I thank Thee, Lord, from the bottom of my heart.

"As You are well aware, my human capacities are at a low ebb. Death and 'him that had the power of death, that is, the devil' [Hebrews 2:14] approach to carry me to the grave. But I refuse to believe that it is my time for death.

"Five years ago You delivered me from death in the hospital. At that time You led me into a special prayer ministry, and I have seen You bless great numbers of people in response to my intercessions on their behalf. I do not believe that You want this work of mine to close at this time.

"You know, Lord, that I am not afraid to die. It is just that I enjoy praying for others so very much, and I see myself as a door opener. One who rushes from prison to prison asking You to release spiritual captives bound in shackles of sin.

"Now, Lord, I am not trying to tell You what to do or how to do it. But as I see it, in 10 days I am scheduled to have surgery. If it is Your will, let Your great power of life permeate my being so that when the surgeon operates he will find no tumor or cancer present.

"Lord, I have so many individuals to pray for that I feel that I must not waste my time praying for myself. I will not speak again of my own physical needs. Instead my prayer is only 'May

Thy will be done in my life, to the glory of the Father, Son, and Holy Spirit.' "

And with that prayer I rested in His love and grace.

On the day of my surgery the orderlies wheeled me into an operating room equipped with the most up-to-date surgical apparatus. Everything shone with a brilliance that spoke of cleanliness and care.

Five hours later I found myself back in my room and feeling fine. Sometime later Dr. Wise came in to see how I was doing. He informed me that he had not found any trace of a tumor. Also, he seemed surprised when I told him that I felt no pain. The patient in the bed next to me had had the same kind of surgery, and he needed injections every so often to relieve the suffering.

The removed tissue went to two different labs to be checked for signs of cancer. Four days later I left the hospital feeling fine and praising God for His great goodness toward me. Another three days went by, and I went to Dr. Wise's office to find out the results of the tests. When I entered, he was all smiles and excited. "No traces of cancer have been found," he reported, then explained how fortunate I was in light of the earlier tests.

Thanking him, I reminded him that after the first tests I had requested to know exactly how critical my situation was. I had wanted to know my condition, I explained, so I would know how I needed to pray. "Now I thank you for being honest with me, and most of all I thank God for doing what was humanly impossible."

Shocking News

About six months later I received a call from California. It was Cyril Grosse, the man who had given me 28 Bible studies in less than a week back in 1946, leading me from spirit worship to Christ. After we had chatted a few minutes, he mentioned that he had some bad news to tell me.

"This may shock you," he said, "but according to my doctor I have only about six months to live. The biopsies have revealed that I have advanced prostate cancer. It has spread to adjoining organs, including the lymph nodes. The doctor says that he will have to do drastic surgery as well as radiation treatments. It may even involve castration."

While the news was bad, it did not throw me into a state of despondency. After all, I had passed through a similar situation only a few months before. God had brought me through it, and I believed that He would do the same for my close friend.

I suggested that he try to postpone the surgery for about three weeks and use the time to enlist the prayers of people he knew to be men and women of strong faith. Of course I added that Hilda and I would also pray for him.

Cyril liked my suggestion, and the doctor went along with his request for a short delay in the surgery. At the end of the three weeks the specialist ran tests that showed a definite improvement in my friend's condition. He told Cyril to return in another three weeks. To the doctor's surprise, the next set of tests showed that a number of the smaller tumors had vanished, and the cancer was in remission.

Every three months Cyril went to the specialist. In October the doctor suggested that the enlarged prostate should be removed in order to restore normal urinary function. The operation was a success, and laboratory analysis revealed only a tiny trace of the cancer remaining in the center of the organ.

Subsequent examinations have shown Cyril to be free of cancer, and my friend is back teaching in his classroom.

A Call for Help

One of my brothers, Edmond, lived in Ottawa. Shortly after *Incredible Answers to Prayer* came off the press, he bought more than 50 copies and sent them to relatives and friends. One copy went to his ex-wife, who lived in Niagara Falls, Ontario.

Impressed by the stories of how God had responded to prayer, she phoned Edmond and asked if he would be willing to contact me and request that I pray about a bone disease that was progressively crippling her.

She had suffered from the painful condition for a number of years. At first a bone deformity had appeared between her ankle and heel, creating a lump that had enlarged to the point that she could no longer wear a shoe. It had also become so painful that she couldn't put any weight on her foot, and had to use crutches.

When the pain became so severe that even powerful medications could no longer block it, the doctors began seriously thinking of amputating her foot. But shortly after I began praying for her, the pain diminished and in a few days vanished completely. The lump began to shrink, and before long she could wear a shoe again.

Since then she has been able to shop and do other activities that people had once been doing for her. She especially appreciated being able to visit some of her children living in northern Ontario.

As I look back upon such experiences in which God has used me to intercede for others, my heart echoes that of the psalmist:

"O give thanks unto the Lord; call
upon his name: make known his deeds
among the people.

"Sing unto him, sing psalms unto
him: talk ye of all his wondrous
works.

"Glory ye in his holy name: let
the heart of them rejoice that seek
the Lord.

"Seek the Lord, and his strength:
seek his face evermore.

"Remember his marvellous works
that he hath done; his wonders,
and the judgments of his mouth"
(Psalm 105:1-5).

CHAPTER

2

No Greater Joy

Since the publication of *Incredible Answers to Prayer* hundreds of individuals have written or telephoned to tell how the Spirit of God has blessed their lives as they read about the power of intercessory prayer and began to put it into practice.

My prayer list has increased by 700 names as I have joined my prayers to their intercessions before God. The Lord has greatly honored us as the Holy Spirit has given people victory over self, over sin, over temptation, and over the power of fallen angels.

And the one thing that most surprises those praying people is how the Spirit of God gets individuals who have no use for God or spiritual things to suddenly have a change of heart. And when such men and women one day sit with them in a Seventh-day Adventist church, they marvel at the power of God to save. God has used their prayers to work miracles. They then write to me long letters telling of the joy they are experiencing.

For example, let me share a few excerpts from letters by a woman I will call Mary Brown.

"Dear Brother Morneau:

"What a joy to serve our Lord in prayer ministry. I have been a baptized Seventh-day Adventist for 15 wonderful years.

How that came about is another thrilling story. During the past two years I have come to believe very strongly in intercessory prayer. Also during that same period I have been seeking a closer walk with Jesus and ways to serve Him more fully each day. He has led and guided me so wonderfully, and your book was a part of that special guidance.

"I have adopted some of your 'proven' ideas. I especially like the one of asking for God to surround my prayer subject with an atmosphere of light and peace. Let me briefly share one prayer experience.

"My sister Josephine, 38 years of age, had an affair, and her husband left as a result. She went through 'hell' (her word) for more than two months after Russell moved out. Although she did not realize it, he had known about the affair for more than a year. She had been pressuring her lover to choose between her or his own wife.

"Up to that time she had never in any way indicated that she felt any need of God or religion. But when this crisis came, she turned to me and asked that I pray for her. I prayed fervently that her lover would stay with his wife. Two months later he emphatically told her that he would never leave his wife, and then ended the affair.

"Some time later I learned that both Josephine and Russell were both praying that they would soon be back together again.

"What a thrill to be used of our dear heavenly Father in such a special work. It is my desire and prayer to become a wise intercessor and to be used more and more by my Master in this precious responsibility. To see how God answers prayer is so exciting. My faith grows steadily. I have adopted the prayer idea you mention on page 48 of your book. What a wonderful, blessing-filled idea.

"The Lord has been good to me. I have several very dear friends, and instead of giving you a few names to place on your prayer list every time I write, I decided to send them all at once. I shall let you know as providence unfolds in each of their lives.

"I have adopted for my personal petition each morning the

beautiful prayer you shared on page 27. . . .

"Today I am mailing a copy of your book to my parents. The Lord has given me wonderful witnessing opportunities with them. They have just recently started going to church (on Sunday), and as Mom put it, they will 'try' different ones to see which they like best. They are truly searching, and as they do, I pray every day. I really believe with all my heart that our Lord will 'bring them in.' It is just a matter of time. That will be a most glorious occasion that I anticipate with great joy.

"I promise to pray for you and yours each day until our dear Jesus comes to take us home. What a blessed, awesome day that will be.

"Have a pleasant, happy day."

Three months later I received another letter from her.

"Dear Brother and Sister Morneau:

"Thank you, Hilda, for your precious note. I have some wonderful prayer answers to share again. If you will recall, I asked you last time to please pray for my sister whose marriage had broken up. They are back together. Her husband came home the week of Christmas, and they are both working to make a go of it. Praise God!

"Another answer to prayer has been the miracle I have seen in my stepdad's life. I don't remember if I told you that he had asked me about the change of worship from Saturday to Sunday, and how I took the opportunity to share the facts with him. Guided by the Holy Spirit, he concluded that Saturday is the Sabbath.

"There have been some evangelistic meetings going on at a town near where they live. I had sent them the brochure, and this past Sunday evening both my mom and Harry came to the meeting. My parents truly enjoyed it. Even Mom, who rarely says much about spiritual matters, commented on what a nice meeting it was.

"My dear dad was beaming. I have noticed a decided change in his countenance since he has embraced the Sabbath. Even three months ago I would have never dreamed that I would be sitting beside my parents in a Seventh-day Adventist church. What a thrill that was. I see before my eyes the working of the Holy Spirit in their lives, and that gives me great courage."

Both letters were actually much longer, telling of other individuals being blessed by the working of the Holy Spirit. When I read or hear of such experiences, I always think of the following quotation from *The Desire of Ages*:

"When the Spirit of God takes possession of the heart, it transforms the life. Sinful thoughts are put away, evil deeds are renounced; love, humility, and peace take the place of anger, envy, and strife. Joy takes the place of sadness, and the countenance reflects the light of heaven" (p. 173).

Each day I grow more excited over the fact that great numbers of church members are pleading for God to extend the merits of Christ's sacrifice to those in need. One person wrote to me, "I became deeply impressed with the importance and great value you are placing on the shed blood of Christ being appropriated to those we pray for. I now take time every day to talk with our heavenly Father about my appreciation of the power to save found in the merits of the divine blood of Christ, and for the Holy Spirit to work out a great salvation in their lives. I am seeing my prayers being answered before my eyes, and that is most wonderful!"

I believe that we are beginning to witness the fulfillment of the words of Isaiah about the closing of God's work in the earth: "Arise, shine; for thy light is come, and the glory of the Lord is risen upon thee. For, behold, the darkness shall cover the earth, and gross darkness the people: but the Lord shall arise upon thee, and his glory shall be seen upon thee. And the gentiles shall come to thy light, and kings to the brightness of thy rising" (Isaiah 60:1-3).

As I read letters from people who are having their intercessory prayers answered, I notice that at the same time they are acquiring a beautiful understanding of how the Holy Spirit "makes effectual what has been wrought out by the world's Redeemer" (*ibid.*, p. 671). They grasp with new clarity that only the Holy Spirit can make and keep the human heart pure.

A number of years ago as I sought a closer walk with Jesus and greater insight into the science of salvation, I came across a passage in volume 8 of *Testimonies for the Church*.

"Christ declared that the divine influence of the Spirit was to be with His followers unto the end. But the promise is not appreciated as it should be; and therefore its fulfillment is not seen as it might be. The promise of the Spirit is a matter little thought of; and the result is only what might be expected—spiritual drought, spiritual darkness, spiritual declension and death. Minor matters occupy the attention, and the divine power which is necessary for the growth and prosperity of the church, and which would bring all other blessings in its train, is lacking, though offered in its infinite plenitude" (p. 21).

For a number of days key phrases of this passage kept repeating themselves in my mind. They drove me to my knees and turned my heart to God for special help. Above all as I read and re-read that last sentence, I deeply felt that I had failed my Saviour. The fact that I would let minor matters crowd out the divine power of the Holy Spirit made me feel almost like a traitor. Then and there I determined that my indifferent attitude would come to an end.

Daily I prayed that God the Father would make me more like Jesus, who "not for Himself, but for others, lived and thought and prayed" (*Christ's Object Lessons*, p. 139). I prayed that I would find my greatest joy in asking the Spirit of God to bless the lives of those whose names were on my perpetual prayer list. Before long I saw the Holy Spirit at work in my life as I frequently thought of those who needed the blessing of God in their lives.

I discovered the joy of praying as I drove my car, as I walked to business calls, as I waited for people who had made appointments with me. And the results delighted me. For example, I would pray for those of my business clients whom I knew were struggling with problems. When I would later visit them, they would spontaneously tell me how God had blessed them.

God's blessing of others continues to this day. Permit me to tell of an experience that had happened just as I was writing this chapter. It was 10:35 on a Friday evening. The sacred hours of the Sabbath had brought a great peace and quiet to our home. Hilda had her attention focused on a good book, and I was thinking about a long-distance telephone call I had received.

A young woman whom I will name Mary had phoned to request that I pray for a friend who had just moments before left her husband for another man. In tears she had told how the friend, whom I will call Betty, had once prayed for her when Mary had had marital problems. In fact, Betty had even contacted me and requested that I pray for Mary. Now it was Mary's turn to seek someone to intercede with God for Betty's salvation.

Although I instantly recognized the name, I let Mary do the talking. Without my prompting her in any way Mary told about the struggles she had gone through. "Jim and I were married a little more than two years and still very much in love," she said. "He was doing graduate study and our income was quite limited, so we were happy when I got a better-paying job that seemed the answer to prayer."

She paused a moment, then asked, "Mr. Morneau, do you think that it is possible for a woman to fall in love with another man even when she is still deeply in love with her husband?"

Instead of slipping into a discussion of genuine love and the power of infatuation, I simply replied that in this day and age many strange things have taken place. "I don't know why I am telling you this," Mary continued, "except that I believe the Holy Spirit wants you to see how the Holy Spirit answered your prayers for me.

"After I had been at my new job in a large department store for a couple months, I began to notice one of the managers. His kindness and habit of complimenting me caught my attention. I began to like him very much.

"Before long I could not get him out of my mind. I found myself thinking about him constantly, even when I was with my husband. Although I realized that it was wrong for me to let him continually occupy my thoughts, I simply couldn't stop it. His power over me was so great that one day I found myself admitting to Betty that if the man asked me to go to bed with him, I would not be able to resist.

"I knew that was exactly what would happen if things kept on going the way they were. Just a few days before, I had discovered myself hoping that he would put his arms around me while we were alone together in a warehouse area.

"At times he had placed a hand on my arm as we talked, and a powerful and most enjoyable sensation had coursed through my entire body. I was getting totally hooked on him. But, thank God, you, Mr. Morneau, and Betty were praying for me. When the day came that he invited me to his apartment to see the stamp collection that was his pride and joy, I automatically replied, 'Oh, I couldn't do that without my husband being with me.'

"Then a tide of fear flooded through my mind as I realized what would take place in his apartment if I were alone with him. A passage I had memorized as a child—Joseph's words when he was faced with temptation—flashed through my mind: 'How then can I do this great wickedness, and sin against God?' Suddenly I was now afraid of something that until that moment I had been longing for.

"I am not exaggerating, Mr. Morneau, when I say that in those few moments I regained my sense of right and wrong. The shackles of infatuation fell off me, and by the grace of God I will never wear them again."

I reminded Mary that people had been making powerful intercessions with God on her behalf. The Holy Spirit had been moving mightily in her time of need. She did not say anything for 10 or 15 seconds, but I could hear her sobbing. Finally, regaining her composure, she thanked me for my prayers for her.

But the reason for her call was still troubling her. She could not understand why the woman who had prayed for her during Mary's time of need should now herself suddenly move in with another man. "How can a person like Betty, one that I always considered to be a strong Christian, fall into sin so totally that she will not listen to reason? Her outlook on life has changed so greatly that spiritual things don't seem to matter to her anymore.

"It scares me when I think of it, and I keep asking myself, 'If

Betty, always before a person of strong principles, can suddenly give up on spiritual things, what chance do I have of making it to heaven?' "

"You are not the only person who has asked me that kind of question," I replied. "In fact, a great number of people have written to me with prayer requests for someone's marriage. People constantly tell me of their shock when they see someone they have considered a pillar of the church suddenly throw his or her marriage away."

A tone of urgency filled her voice as she asked me what I thought was happening to the church. I explained that I believed that such people had not learned how to be "kept by the power of God through faith" (1 Peter 1:5), and that the widespread adultery and marital breakup among Adventists was the consequence of church members slowly releasing their hold upon God until the natural inclinations of the fallen human heart overwhelmed them.

The book *Patriarchs and Prophets*, I said, describes three distinct factors that caused the ancient Israelites to abandon God. "It was when the Israelites were in a condition of outward ease and security that they were led into sin. They *failed* to keep God ever before them, they *neglected* prayer and *cherished* a spirit of self-confidence" (p. 459; italics supplied). Ellen White then goes on in pages 459 through 461 to warn us that what caused God's people to apostatize at the river Jordan will also be prevalent before the second coming of Christ.

"Turning away from something as sacred as wedding vows," I told her, "makes no sense unless we remember that the fallen human 'heart is deceitful above all things, and desperately wicked' [Jeremiah 17:9]. In fact, it is so deceptive that even Solomon, the wisest of all human beings and thrice called by Scripture beloved of God, ruined his life when he forgot to keep God always before him. He soon discovered the power of unbridled infatuation. The Bible says that 'his wives turned away his heart after other gods. . . . Then did Solomon build an high place for Chemosh, the abomination of Moab, in the hill that is before Jerusalem, and for Molech. . . . And likewise did he for all his strange wives, which burnt incense and sacrificed unto their gods' [1 Kings 11:4-8]."

Mary wanted to know more about being "kept by the power of God through faith." I promised to write a letter in which I would explain about the power of sin and separation from God, and how helpless we are against such forces unless the Spirit of God intervenes.

In the chapters to follow I will present some of the important factors that we need to know to preserve our vital relationship with God. Also, I will show how our prayers for another can allow God to send the Holy Spirit more fully to fight our loved ones' battles against sin and evil.

CHAPTER

3

Self-bashing Parents

Of the vast numbers of letters and prayer requests that I receive, one particular type never fails to touch my emotions deeply. They come from God-loving parents whose children have rejected their faith and church. And I believe that I can say without exaggeration that 7 out of every 10 of those parents feel that they are somehow to blame for what their children have done. Almost everyone seems to write, "As parents we wonder where we have gone wrong in bringing up our children. Where have we failed them?"

Some of those parents are so crushed by their disappointment that they withdraw from contact with other church members for fear of having to explain about their children. One mother unloaded her burden of cares, then asked me to pray especially for her husband. His life had been so devastated by the way their adult children lived that he no longer went to church. He could not face his fellow believers there.

She feared that it would not take much more before he killed himself. "I wish that I were dead," he had told her a number of times. "Then I would not have to live such a life of misery."

When I write back to Christian parents going through such experiences, I emphasize that they should not blame themselves for what their children may be doing. No parent is ever perfect, but even more important to remember is that young people make their own free choices. It is the devil who attempts to lay on these parents guilt for what someone else—particularly their children—do or don't do. Why not place the blame where it really belongs—on the person's own fallen, sinful heart? Each individual chooses to follow his or her own evil inclinations as well as those of the devil and his evil angels.

Satan seeks to coerce us into accepting unnecessary blame and guilt. When I participated in spirit worship many years ago, a spirit priest claimed that after someone's spouse dies, demon spirits find great delight in bringing to the mind of the grieving husband or wife all the unkindness that he or she ever did over the years to the departed loved one.

Evil angels bombard each suffering person with images of guilt and regret in order to discourage and even crush the joy of living from him or her. "This kind of mental oppression greatly pleases Satan," that spirit worshiper said. And I believe that we must consider seriously what he taught. It echoes what Scripture says about Satan's lust to destroy like a roaring lion. If he can't tempt us into rejecting God by doing wrong, he will try to destroy us by paralyzing us with false guilt.

Self-bashing parents need to heed Jesus' invitation to "come unto me, all ye that labour and are heavy laden, and I will give you rest" (Matthew 11:28). Our Lord offers to endow us with endurance, that special capacity that will keep us going in difficult times, when everyone else's life is falling apart.

As I stated earlier, I have received countless letters from parents on the point of despair over their children. But after they begin to realize that the Holy Spirit can work mighty miracles of redemption, those same parents start writing me about how the Lord has been blessing their families. They tell how the Spirit's power is transforming lives and remedying desperate situations. Those letters record victories in what have appeared to be hopeless cases.

"It is with a heavy heart that I write you," one letter began. "I know that God is not partial when He seems to answer some people's prayers more than others. However, I feel that my prayers are ineffectual because I do not see the answers I desire.

"I am not praying for money, houses, or earthly goods. Our requests are for our children. We have one son and one daughter. The problems are chiefly these.

"Our daughter, Darlene, lies and is very manipulative. She is also very belligerent, ignores our rules, and has no regard for God.

"Our son, Charles, lacks the motivation to make a life for himself. He is careless about his lessons, gets depressed easily, and at the least problem gives in and becomes extremely uncommunicative. Charles attended one of our SDA colleges, but did not do well. Our home is in constant turmoil.

"Brother Morneau, perhaps these problems do not seem like life-shattering ones, but we can see that if our son and daughter continue the way they are going, the devil will soon have them where he wants them. While I'm not trying to make it appear we were 'perfect' people, we have tried to set a good example for them: worship, faithful church attendance, the whole nine yards. And I must say, God has been good to us. But the way things are going with our young people, at times the pressures become unbearable.

"We are drowning under these pressures, Brother Morneau. We desperately need help in presenting them to God. Please put us on your prayer list, please!"

In a similar letter the writer quoted her husband as saying, "I feel that any more pressure being brought into my life by our ungodly children will drive me to kill myself."

Such words of desperation always bring tears to my eyes and an ache to my heart. Therefore, after presenting each case before the Lord, I try to reply to the parents in a way that will bring a spark of hope into their lives. I want them to see that through our heavenly Father's perfect plan of redemption, the Holy Spirit can wonderfully change even the most discouraging situation. The Holy Spirit will exalt Christ and reveal Him for the mighty Saviour that He is.

People seem thrilled that anyone will take the time to respond to their hurting. The mother of Darlene and Charles wrote back, "When I received and read your letter it was such a joy—even more so because it was unexpected." Countless people are hoping that someone else will share just a little of their burden, will at least be willing to listen to their grief and hurt if nothing else.

About two months later the woman sent me a letter telling me of remarkable changes taking place in the two young adults. Her letter was full of thanksgiving for God's blessings.

Darlene, the daughter, had transformed from a belligerent, antireligious young woman to a courteous, considerate person who now attended church and was eager to talk about her new interest in spiritual matters. She even stated that she was praying for the Lord to change her.

The son, Charles, had also acquired a new outlook on life. Instead of lacking motivation and being careless in his studies, he now enjoyed college and would tackle problems with new vigor. He also told his mother that he had stopped smoking and engaging in other habits that he had picked up.

Because the mother was a professional working for an international firm, she knew that she did not have as much time as she would have liked to write me about the changes in her family's life. Instead she asked for my telephone number, and since then has called as well as written to keep me posted on what has been happening in her life. No longer depressed and discouraged, she has been joyous as she has told me what the Holy Spirit has been doing in the lives of the people she and her husband have been praying for. They see the Spirit of God imparting to helpless human beings the power to live successful, victorious Christian lives.

Facing Reality

The power of evil has been strengthening for centuries and has now reached the point that it overwhelms reason and parental authority as it devastates Christian homes. But I refuse to accept the widespread notion that there isn't much one can do except ask the Lord to watch over erring loved ones. We can claim the merits of the blood Christ shed at Calvary. And if we understand how that divine power can be enlisted for the salvation of those who have departed from

God, we can expect mighty miracles of redemption to take place in the lives of those we pray for.

Before we examine how divine power can transform lives, I believe we first need to consider the immensity of the sin problem in our lives. Three powerful evil elements seek control of each one of us, elements that without God's strength we are defenseless against. They are:

1. The power of sin.
2. The power of death.
3. The power of separation from God.

Jesus has enumerated some of the evils that **the power of sin** can produce in an individual's life: "From within, out of the heart of men, proceed evil thoughts, adulteries, fornications, murders, thefts, covetousness, wickedness, deceit, lasciviousness, an evil eye, blasphemy, pride, foolishness: All these evil things come from within, and defile the man" (Mark 7:21-23). It is no wonder that the Bible declares that the human heart "is deceitful above all things, and desperately wicked" (Jeremiah 17:9).

A number of letters have come to me from Christian men who were distressed by the impure thoughts that flooded their minds. They discover that their efforts to rechannel their thoughts to good things is a constant struggle.

"I am almost discouraged over the fact that as soon as I wake up in the morning, I find myself thinking about some of the immoralities that I did before becoming a Christian," one individual wrote. "I try very hard to think on good things, but before long some of those corrupt imaginations are back again. And the sad part of it all is that at times I find myself thinking upon those with greedy interest.

"I often wonder if I am fighting a losing battle here?

"Is there any way of beating this thing?

"Or do you think that I am a hopeless case?

"When I read Psalm 24, verses 3 and 4 ["Who shall ascend into the hill of the Lord? or who shall stand in his holy place? He that hath clean hands, and a pure heart"], I feel that I will miss out on eternal life because I don't have a pure heart as mentioned here."

In my reply I stated that nothing short of the divine power of Christ dispensed daily through the Holy Spirit could bring him victory. Then I told him about a time-tested formula that for decades has kept sin from separating me from Jesus. Six months went by; then the man wrote me the good news that he was having a closer walk with God. He praised God for the fact that He could transform his life by the Holy Spirit.

The power of death drives many people to smoke, drink alcohol, use drugs, or adopt a lifestyle that will shorten life. They ignore scientific evidence of the dangers of such habits and practices and refuse to listen to reason or common sense.

Others struggle with the compulsion to take risks. The greater the danger, the more powerful the high they get from it. I believe it is one of the reasons young people have so many deadly car accidents. During the 1980s car crashes killed more than 74,000 teenagers in the United Sates. Many of the survivors relate how an inner force compelled them to drive recklessly.

As we analyze **the power of separation from God**, we find that it consists of two distinct elements: distrust of God and unbelief. It has wrecked untold millions of lives through the centuries. The antediluvians refused to enter Noah's ark, and the Hebrews who left Egypt perished in the wilderness rather than enter the Land of Promise.

Besides the self-destructive forces that lurk within each one of us, we must also remember that Satan and his fallen followers are also doing everything they can to distress, perplex, and oppress our minds and lives.

By now our hearts would sink in despair were it not for the fact that our mighty Redeemer, Jesus Christ, can save completely from self, from sin, from the world, and from the power of fallen angels. Jesus can do what we cannot, can protect us from that which we would be defenseless against, and can transform us into what we would never be otherwise. He is the only hope that we can ever have.

CHAPTER

4

Unlimited Help

Christ's return is too near for us to continue to waste time in the hopeless pursuit of trying to earn our own salvation. Instead we must spend our time in prayer seeking the Holy Spirit, that great power through whom alone we can resist and overcome sin (*The Desire of Ages*, p. 671). On that same page Ellen White tells us that Jesus gives His Spirit as a "divine power to overcome all hereditary or cultivated tendencies to evil, and to impress His own character upon this church."

Living victorious and successful Christian lives is the all-important thing, and we can do it only one way—through the Spirit of God resting upon us and dwelling in us.

The apostle Paul, writing to the Ephesians for whose salvation he had labored so diligently, caught their attention by stressing the kind of prayer he did for them. "For this cause I bow my knees unto the Father of our Lord Jesus Christ, . . . that he would grant you, according to the riches of his glory, to be strengthened with might by his Spirit in the inner man; that Christ may dwell in your hearts by faith; that ye, being rooted and grounded in love, may be able to comprehend with all saints what is the breadth, and length, and depth, and height; and to know the love of Christ, which passeth knowledge, that ye might be filled with all the fulness of God" (Ephesians 3:14-19).

Those few lines must have been a wonderful encouragement to the Christians at Ephesus as they realized that Paul had been praying for the Holy Spirit to strengthen them in a special way. Only then could they live victorious Christian lives in this fallen world.

To understand the impact that Paul's prayer had on them we must remember that the Ephesians had at one time been anything but model individuals. Ephesians 2:1, 2 declared of them, "And you hath he quickened, who were dead in trespasses and sins; wherein in time past ye walked according to the course of this world, according to the prince of the power of the air, the spirit that now worketh in the children of disobedience."

A number of the Ephesians had even been deeply involved in the supernatural. Acts 19:19 tells us, "Many of them also which used curious arts brought their books together, and burned them before all men; and they counted the price of them, and found it to be fifty thousand pieces of silver."

Convicted by the Holy Spirit, these practitioners of the occult burned manuscripts worth a fortune and yielded their lives to Christ. I can imagine that Paul and his 12 companions (mentioned at the beginning of the chapter) must have done some serious praying for these men and women.

I believe that they prayed both for God to appropriate the merits of the blood Christ shed at Calvary, and for the Spirit of God to surround each one with a divine atmosphere of peace and spiritual light. And it could well be that they asked God to have the Holy Spirit overpower and nullify the power of sin, the power of death, and the power of separation from God in each believer's life. Surely Paul and his friends must have made this kind of prayer daily.

Fantastic conversions took place among the Ephesians, and I am persuaded by the Word of God that similar and far more numerous conversions will happen among the Seventh-day Adventist Church when God's people intercede with God for others with a faith as determined as that Paul and his friends had.

In 1946, after the Holy Spirit converted me from spiritualism to Christianity, the Epistle to the Ephesians became a great source of encouragement to me—especially when I realized what Paul's prayer had accomplished among those who had been involved in the occult. Ephesians 2:4-7 has never failed to amaze me. "But God, who is rich in mercy, for his great love wherewith he loved us, even when we were dead in sins, hath quickened us together with Christ, (by grace ye are saved;) . . . that in the ages to come he might show the exceeding riches of his grace in his kindness toward us through Christ Jesus." We will be the demonstration and showcase before the rest of the universe of His forgiveness and ability to transform rebellious sinners.

Grace took on even greater meaning one day when I read that it is a fundamental part of God's character. Ellen White says that it "is an attribute of God exercised toward undeserving human beings. We did not seek for it, but it was sent in search of us. God rejoices to bestow His grace upon us, not because we are worthy, but because we are so utterly unworthy. Our only claim to His mercy is our great need" (*The Ministry of Healing*, p. 161).

The Spirit of God strengthened the early Christians, enabling them to become something they otherwise could not. It alone empowered them to live successful Christian lives. And according to the apostle John, heaven blessed their prayer life, the secret of their victorious Christianity. "Whatsoever we ask, we receive of him, because we keep his commandments, and do those things that are pleasing in his sight" (1 John 3:22). They were able to keep His commandments because their prayer life opened up to them the power of the Holy Spirit, as we witness over and over in the New Testament.

Acts 3 records how Peter and John visited the Temple in Jerusalem at the daily hour of prayer. As they approached one of the gates a lame beggar stopped them and asked them for money. "Then Peter said, Silver and gold have I none; but such as I have give I thee: In the name of Jesus Christ of Nazareth rise up and walk" (verse 6). The Bible states that the crippled man's feet and ankles received healing and strength, and he began to leap and praise God.

It is my firm conviction that God will again demonstrate such miracles among His people, but right now we are still in the process of acquiring genuine biblical faith. Such faith is a must before He can honor our prayers as He did the disciples and other early Christians. According to Hebrews 11, such biblical faith consists of three elements:

1. Belief in God.
2. Trust in God.
3. Loyalty to God.

Jesus—Lord of the Impossible

Shortly after the publication of my book on intercessory prayer, a woman wrote, "I have a son that needs the kind of praying that you talked about in your book. I would like very much to talk to you about him, if you would be kind enough to send me your phone number. It would be so much easier to tell you about his problem over the phone. Please help me! A sister in Christ."

A few days later I received a phone call from her. She explained that she and her husband had a 32-year-old son named Henry who by the age of 20 had apparently lost almost all his mental faculties because of drug use. Since then he had been unable to take care of himself. He would sit in a chair for as long as three hours at a time, silently smoking and staring at a wall. Sometimes Henry's eyes would follow his mother as she cooked or moved around the kitchen. The son had no sense of day or night, and when he did sleep, it was only for short periods of time. Occasionally he would slap himself with great force in the face or on his arms or legs until he turned black and blue.

When told not to hurt himself, Henry would explode into rage and insist that no one should speak to him. He had let his hair grow down to the middle of his back, refusing to allow anyone to cut it. The man seemed unable to recognize even his parents, and his speech was unintelligible. At times he would talk to himself in a series of grunts. His parents considered his condition hopeless.

After I had listened to Mrs. Harvey (not her real name) for about 20 minutes, I began to wonder why she was asking me for help in a situation that appeared even beyond the aid of medical science. Then I realized that it wasn't me that mattered here, but God. The woman was trying to reach out to God through me. Perhaps the Lord could use me to lead her to the Holy Spirit and His life-giving power. Perhaps the Holy Spirit was waiting to re-create the son's mental faculties, thereby exalting Christ and strengthening the faith of many.

Silently I asked God to bless my mind with what I should say to her. After conversing with her awhile, I assured her that I would take Henry's case to heart. I would place his name on my prayer list and pray for him in a special way. Also I requested that she periodically keep me posted on his condition.

Time went by, and one day I received a letter from her telling me that Henry was beginning to improve. His speech had become clearer, and—to his parents' surprise—he asked his mother to cut his hair for the first time in 16 years. Mrs. Harvey was elated, and she stated that her and her husband's faith was growing stronger as they saw the Spirit of God blessing their son's life.

Offering my own thanksgiving to God, I pointed her to biblical incidents in which the Lord had done wonderful things for His people. Most of all I emphasized the fact that God "longs to have [us] reach after Him by faith. He longs to have [us] expect great things from Him" (*Christ's Object Lessons*, p. 146).

A few months later Henry decided to stop smoking. When he announced his intention, his mother figured that because he had been a chain smoker for so many years, he would be unable to quit. She had known too many people who had tried and failed.

But to his parents' astonishment, Henry never touched a cigarette again. Mrs. Harvey waited a month before writing me about it. For the next six or seven months she sent me a monthly report, and to my joy she and her husband gave God all the credit for all the changes in their son's life. Yet one thing still bothered her—God wasn't restoring his mind as they had hoped for. One additional letter arrived. In it Mrs. Harvey admitted that her faith in God's power to help them was beginning to waver. Naturally I prayed that her faith would not fail her.

When we seek a special blessing from God, the Bible says, "Let him ask in faith, nothing wavering. For he that wavereth is like a wave of the sea driven with the wind and tossed. For let not that man think that he shall receive any thing of the Lord" (James 1:6, 7).

About 11:00 in the evening not more than 10 days later Mrs. Harvey called me. She could barely talk because of crying. With a quick silent prayer for help, I managed to calm her down to the point where I could make out what she was saying. It seemed that Henry had unexpectedly become violent, throwing chairs through the windows and threatening to beat up his father. They had had to call the sheriff's department and have the son taken to a mental institution. She informed me that she had lost all hope of her son ever getting better. "I am sorry to tell you this," she said, "but I have lost faith in the power of prayer, and will no longer trouble God with my needs."

Telling her not to give up, I said that I would redouble my intercessions for her son. I believed that his violent reaction had been brought on by the forces of darkness. They were trying to get us to quit praying for Henry. Before she hung up I left her with a few verses of Scripture to think about.

It wasn't many days later that she called again. This time her voice vibrated with happiness as she praised God for a mighty miracle of divine grace. Henry was back home healthy both in mind and body. Although he could remember nothing that had taken place during the past 12 years, he was out visiting old friends, neighbors, and relatives with his father.

When I asked Mrs. Harvey how it had happened, she said her son had awakened one morning at the mental institution feeling perfectly well. The doctors found him mentally alert, and after a day or two phoned his parents to come get their wonderfully transformed son.

"Glory to God in the highest!" I shouted over the phone, and rejoiced with her over how God still shows His love for us.

CHAPTER

5

The Tragedy of Crumbling Homes

A spiritual plague has been devastating the lives of men, women, and children around the world. It afflicts both young and old, but especially brings misery to innocent children who can't begin to understand why mother and dad can no longer get along, and one of them is now moving out.

The past couple decades have seen a climate that desensitizes the mind to one's responsibilities as a spouse and parent. Satan and his angels are working with all the various forces of today's society to destroy the natural affection that the Creator planted in each human being. They permeate our culture with sexual imagery and expose everyone to all kinds of immorality.

Long ago Ellen White revealed how Satan works to destroy the family and every other God-ordained relationship. "Satan is using every means to make crime and debasing vice popular. We cannot walk the streets of our cities without encountering flaring notices of crime presented in some novel, or to be acted at some theater. The mind is educated to familiarity with sin.

"The course pursued by the base and vile is kept before the people in the periodicals of the day, and everything that can excite passion is brought before them in exciting stories. They hear and read so much of debasing crime that the once tender conscience, which would have recoiled with horror from such scenes, becomes hardened, and they dwell upon these things with greedy interest" (*Patriarchs and Prophets*, p. 459).

Today television and other media have offered additional channels for Satan to do his work. In this day and age, unless a person makes constant and determined daily requests for God's help to remain pure in thought, heart, and life, even the most self-disciplined individual may imperceptibly become corrupt at heart, and suddenly fall like a rotten oak tree. Permit me to illustrate.

"My husband and I are in our 50s," a woman wrote to me one day, "have raised a family, worked hard to educate our children, and brought them up in the admonition of the Lord. Our grown children have married well, have established homes that are under the blessing of God. I have always been committed to church activities, and enjoyed serving the Lord.

"My husband was first elder of our large church, and lived what we all thought was an exemplary life. He was looked upon as a pillar in the church until about six months ago when it was discovered that he had been secretly enjoying a girlie magazine and pornographic videotapes.

"His evil interest was revealed in the following way. Friends of ours who live in a rural area had been having difficulties with their 20-year-old daughter who was attending a community college. They had discussed the problem with us, and we agreed that Reta (not her name) could live with us, where she could then attend an SDA college.

"All went well until one evening I attended a Community Services meeting that ended about an hour earlier than usual. Arriving home, I unexpectedly found my husband in bed with Reta. Since then the whole thing has been like a nightmare.

"My husband has moved to another area, is still shacking up with that innocent-looking girl, and has just informed me that he wants a divorce. He is a changed man, but not for the better. Now he doesn't care about me, about the church, not even about the fact that he has hurt the lives of a great many persons. It is too bad that such a thing took place in our lives. We had reached the point where there were no longer any college tuition bills to meet, no real problems to worry about. My husband and I had been able to set aside quite a lot of money for our retirement, and were looking forward to enjoying the golden years of our lives.

"The thing that makes it so difficult to adjust to my great loss is that my husband had been a man of principle all through his life. I considered him to be as solid as the Rock of Gibraltar when it came to standing firmly for right. It is sad to say, but I was wrong.

"Our two married sons have stopped going to church, and that has brought great distress to the lives of their wives and children."

The woman, after giving me additional information on the problem, requested that I pray for each member of her family. She is hurting and wonders if she could have done anything prayerwise to avert such a tragedy.

In another case a wife wrote how her 60-year-old husband had gotten sexually involved with their 17-year-old foster daughter. Again the husband moved out and is living together with the girl. Head deacon in his church, he greatly shocked many people by his actions. His wife wondered if he could suddenly have become mentally unbalanced. She asked that I pray for all three involved, because she still wants her husband to be in Christ's kingdom. And she too, like so many others who have had such tragedies strike them, wondered if there was a particular way she could have prayed to prevent such a thing happening in her husband's life.

Before I explain what I term *preventative praying*, I would like to say that over the years I have been an attentive student of human nature. I have always been interested in knowing what compels a person to do something that he or she later deeply regrets. For 20 years I was in telephone directory (yellow pages) advertising sales. Year after year I would call back on the same businesspeople, and they learned to trust me and often began to confide their problems to me.

From what they told me about their lives, I discovered that though a man may have been brought up to practice self-control and to be temperate in all things, when the media,

Satan, or anything else begins to influence his imagination toward an attractive female, it will not take long before he is willing to risk all, to throw everything away, to indulge in his fantasies.

A spiritist priest once claimed to me that demon spirits can flash thought images into people's minds to influence them in a particular direction. How Satan could do this we do not know, but we all recognize how evil influences—whatever their source—sway people. If men (and women) start dwelling upon such evil suggestions, they soon start creating a bright and exciting picture in their minds of what it would be like if only they put that idea into practice.

The more a person plays with the idea or suggestion, the more powerful and realistic it becomes. Soon it can take control of the mind to the point where an individual will find himself or herself doing things he or she knows shouldn't be done. Demon spirits or other influences can take control of the life until nothing on the human level can break the hold.

Because of the deceptive power of sin a Christian spouse should be willing to do some serious *preventative praying* regardless of how faithful the husband or wife has been to his or her marriage vows. No matter how noble a Christian one has been, it is still possible to fall. Even Satan was a sinless being.

Every day it is good to thank God for having blessed a loved one with grace and strength, for having imparted to him or her divine compassionate love. Only when a person possesses the love of Christ can he or she display toward a fellow human being the heavenly graces that adorn the character of our great Redeemer.

The spouse who wants to spend eternity with his or her husband, as well as have him or her in the present life, must secure the stabilizing influence of the Holy Spirit, that great divine power that alone can impart purity of thought, heart, and life. While God never forces anyone to do anything against his or her will, He will, because of the merits of the blood Christ shed on the cross, do everything possible to protect and lead a person toward salvation. Christ tells us always to "pray one for another."

Over the past few years many letters have arrived from husbands and wives in shaky marriages. After I have shared with them these principles, the Spirit of God administered to their spouses the graces of redemption and solidified their union in Christ. Nothing can be more rewarding than to hear again from those same individuals how the Lord has blessed in joyous and surprising ways.

Lost and Found

Here is an outstanding illustration of how the stabilizing influence of the Holy Spirit can restore spiritually wayward individuals.

Shortly after *Incredible Answers* came off the press, I received a letter from a woman whose husband had left her almost four years before. She was particularly impressed by the fact that before I pray for a person who does not serve God, I first ask that the Father will appropriate the merits of Christ's blood to the person in need, always conscious that the individual's redemption has already been paid for.

"When I read in your book that we can pray for the Lord to forgive another's sins," she said, "I was astounded, and began praying for my husband with new faith and hope."

She said that she and her husband were both in their thirties, had good jobs and health, and had looked forward to a bright future. Employed by a multinational corporation, the man spoke three languages which quickly propelled him up the corporate ladder.

"Before long the demands of the job began to take him away from home days at a time. It wasn't long before the lavish lifestyle of the corporate world began making its mark on him. Even his character was changing in that he became quite critical of me, and seemed to be looking for occasions to disagree on most everything I said.

"He began to criticize the church and its people, and the time came that I found myself going to church alone. As time passed he began wearing expensive jewelry, and not long after I became aware that he was smoking. And when he was brought home drunk from a Christmas party, he added to my disappointment by stating that he was also having an affair with his secretary.

"Our home became a place of contention and unrest. At that time I thanked the Lord that we didn't have any children to be torn apart by the terrible discord. I did all I could to have us seek the help of an SDA counselor, but to no avail. In fact, he moved out and blamed me for breaking up our home."

In a telephone conversation she told me that she didn't hear about him for almost two years. Then she found out that he was in deep trouble with his employer. He had made several decisions that had caused the corporation to lose vast amounts of money. Before long the company terminated him, and he left the area so that she lost track of him. His experience at the multinational corporation now made it impossible to obtain similar employment, which drove him to heavy drinking.

Later she found out that he tried gambling and was successful at it for a time. Next he got involved in drugs, causing him to lose control of his life and everything he possessed. He thought of killing himself, "but discovered that he didn't have what it took to carry on with his plan. That was most shocking to his manhood to realize that he was some kind of coward," his wife told me.

Meanwhile she acquired a copy of my book, read it, and was especially impressed with the chapter "Praying for the Ungodly and the Wicked." She wrote to ask if I would join her in praying for her husband whom she hoped was still alive.

I wrote back to assure her that the Holy Spirit would surely minister the graces of redemption to the man as she and I sought God's help. Ellen White tells us that Satan and his angels are "redoubling their efforts to defeat the work of Christ in man's behalf, and to fasten souls in their snares. To hold the people in darkness and impenitence till the Saviour's mediation is ended, and there is no longer a sacrifice for sin, is the object which they seek to accomplish" (*The Great Controversy*, p. 518). But she also reminds us again and again that God seeks to end such bondage.

Knowing what both the demons and Christ were determined to do in this man's life, I became bolder in my determination that Satan would not have his way, but that Christ would. With this man, as with everyone else I pray for, I relied on the mighty power of the Holy Spirit to overpower, and render nonoperative, the enemies of Jesus Christ and all those He is determined to save.

I assured the woman that I would put both her and her husband's name on my perpetual prayer list. Daily and without fail I would present them before Jesus. I asked only that she keep me posted on what was happening in their lives.

About a year went by. Then one evening she had on the national television news as it interviewed a group of homeless people in a distant city. The people were living in the back of an abandoned factory under a highway overpass. The state wanted to demolish their shacks and move them elsewhere.

As she was cooking, she heard a familiar voice. Turning around, she saw her husband on the screen. If he had not spoken, she would have never recognized him. He wore a beard and had long hair down his back and, she said, "looked like a tramp. He was a pitiful sight."

When he stated that he obtained most of his food from the garbage cans behind restaurants, she burst into tears. It broke her heart. Despite her deep sorrow, she was thankful that he was still alive, and that fact gave her hope of better things to come.

The next day she contacted the news network and learned where the interview had been done. Arranging to have some time off from work, she began her search for her husband.

But some time later as she steered her car between shacks and old broken-down machinery to reach a group of men warming themselves by a fire in a steel barrel, she began to worry about her safety and made sure that her car was carefully locked.

One of the men told her what shack to go to, adding that it had no door. She would have to wedge her way between a large piece of heavy canvas and the shack to reach the opening.

The woman found her husband in his 8- x 10-foot shack, lying on a pile of broken-down cardboard boxes about 20 inches in height that he used to insulate himself from the cold of the pavement. As he got up to let some more light into the place, she threw herself into his arms, saying, "I will never let you go!"

Stunned by her action, he kept repeating, "Please let me go. I am filthy—I am disgustingly filthy."

It was late autumn in that distant eastern city, and a light snow was falling. Getting cold, she invited him to sit with her in her car. Refusing to enter the car lest he dirty it, he stood by the door while she kept the window partly down. As the snow continued to fall, he soon resembled a snow man.

Would he sit in the car if she covered the seat with a blanket? she asked. When he said he would, she drove off, to return 45 minutes later with a car blanket and an abundance of hot food from a fast food restaurant. The sight of him feasting on what he considered food fit for a king brought joy to her heart. Silently she sent a melody of praise ascending to God for bringing her husband back into her life. She believed that God was marvelously answering her prayers.

It took a whole week of talking before he agreed to resume living with her. She discovered that once a person's life has deteriorated to the degree his had, only special divine grace can transform it back again.

When at the end of the first day she had not succeeded in getting him out of his shack, she returned to her motel. That evening she did much praying, and sought special guidance on how to handle the situation. She desperately wanted him to resume a normal life again. As she told me later, she reread large portions of *Incredible Answers to Prayer* to fortify herself in the power and love of God. Then, before retiring for the night, she opened her Bible for something to meditate upon. Glancing down at the right-hand page, her eyes fell upon the following words:

"If the Spirit of him that raised up Jesus from the dead dwell in you, he that raised up Christ from the dead shall also quicken your mortal bodies by his Spirit that dwelleth in you" (Romans 8:11).

"That's it," she said to herself. "My husband's mind needs to be re-created by the power of the Spirit of God to what it once was—to the degree of sanity that he once possessed."

Down on her knees she went, pouring out her heart to God.

Five days passed, and everything seemed at a standstill. Then an idea entered her mind. *What my husband needs is to hear of God's power and love operating in people's behalf in these modern times. I will read him portion's of* Morneau's *book.*

That she did, and God began to work through those feeble words. Slowly he began to respond to the Spirit and her suggestions that she and he could still have a bright future together if they would make God first in their lives.

"I couldn't stop the tears from running down my face as I listened to him talk, and realized that the Holy Spirit was bringing my husband back from the dead. He had died spiritually, and now he was alive again, telling me of the joy that he once had when serving God."

Then she received the shock of her life when he said, "OK, Linda (not her real name), I accept your invitation for us to live once again as husband and wife. That is, if you can get transferred by your company to a city where no one knows us. I couldn't face people who knew me in the past. Meanwhile you will have me stay a few miles out of town—am I right?"

Again she assured him that she would do all that she had promised earlier. It took another couple of days to persuade him to go to a barber shop, to clothing stores, and to clean himself up so that he could live like a normal person once more.

So it was by the mighty outworkings of the Holy Spirit that Linda obtained a transfer to another city, and to her great surprise, it was a promotion that involved a substantial increase in pay. Both are now living happily together in the Lord. Both their Christian walks have, she says, matured under the nurturing of the Spirit of God.

Private people, Linda had once asked me that I never tell anyone about her husband's experience. I had promised to abide by her wishes. However, more recently I began to feel that I should ask permission to include it in this book as a means of exalting our Saviour's love and power. They agreed as long as I did not mention their names or where the events had taken place. I believe their experience gives glory to God in the highest!

CHAPTER

6

A Prayer Ministry

Perhaps the question people most ask me is "How can a person begin a successful prayer ministry and keep it going? One that will enable me to actually see my prayers answered?"

I have discovered five steps to follow that have demonstrated that they will bring the power of God into the lives of those you pray for.

Step 1: The key to any successful prayer ministry begins with having a closer walk with Jesus. He is the chief soul winner, and longs to help each one of us to share in His mission. For me that walk with Jesus begins as soon as I open my eyes in the morning, even before I get out of bed. My morning prayer goes something like this:

"Precious Jesus, Thou Lord of glory, I am looking up to the Holy of Holies of the heavenly sanctuary where You are ministering in behalf of fallen humanity, and I seek from Your hand at the beginning of this day a fresh unction of Your love and grace.

"As You are well aware, Lord, my fallen nature is such that if left to myself I will only produce all kinds of wicked deeds that would lead to my eternal destruction. Therefore, I cry unto Thee, Lord, please appropriate to me at this moment the merits of the blood that You shed at Calvary for the remission of sins.

"I wish for You to mold me, to fashion me, to raise me into a pure and holy atmosphere where the rich currents of Your love may flow through my soul, and in turn bless those I encounter in this land of Your enemy.

"I pray, precious Redeemer, for Thy Holy Spirit to rest upon me, and to dwell in me this day, and to make me like Thyself in character. Thank You for being attentive to my prayers. Amen."

After getting up and attending to my early morning needs—such as letting the dog out, etc.—I then have my devotions. They usually consist of reading the Bible and some other inspiring material that will lead me to additional conversation in prayer with Jesus. Only then do I present before Him my prayer list (which by now has filled up a 150-page record book).

Each name in the list has an accompanying description of his or her needs. While it is impossible to mention every person individually, each day I do present a great number by name as the Spirit of God brings them to my attention. But I pray for the great spiritual needs of all my people in the way that I believe that the apostle Paul prayed for the church members at Ephesus (see chapter 4).

After breakfast I converse in prayer with my heavenly Father, praising His name, and giving thanks for the infinite mercies He has showered upon the lives of those I have been praying for. I appreciate and thank God for the fact that I am retired and thus have so much time to carry on my prayer ministry.

Step 2: A solid foundation is a must if one expects to erect any edifice that will be able to stand the test of time. The same principle applies to the spiritual realm. To build an unfaltering trust in God and in the power of His Holy Spirit, we must memorize the Word of God. We must fill our minds with scriptures that will encourage, inspire, uplift, and, above all, draw one's heart to Him. As we do this, we open the way for the Holy Spirit later to bring them to mind in times of need. The

Word of God is a divine avenue of power and life.

I am speaking here from experience. Over the past 46 years I have carried in my coat pocket pieces of paper upon which I have copied verses of Scripture to memorize during my leisure time. During that time I have committed more than 2,200 verses to memory, immeasurably enriching my spiritual life. I invite you to steep yourself in Scripture. If you do, you will produce prayers that will pay high dividends in souls.

Step 3: Compassionate love motivated Christ to come to this rebellious planet and let wicked men nail Him to a cross—all so He could obtain eternal life for each one of us. "He who by a command could bring the heavenly host to His aid—He who could have driven the mob in terror from His sight by the flashing forth of His divine majesty—submitted with perfect calmness to the coarsest insult and outrage" (*The Desire of Ages*, p. 734).

In other words, Christ had a love for His children that was boundless. Jesus was a caring person in the fullest sense of the term. He wants you and me to share that same compulsion. We need to pray with the greatest possible intensity and desire that He will endow us with that same motivating force.

Step 4: To pray for others, we must absolutely have a living faith. Christ's statement "When the Son of man cometh, shall he find faith on the earth?" (Luke 18:8) suggests that it may be a rare experience during the last days, but successful prayer for others is impossible without it.

As we read the four Gospels, we soon notice that the measure of the miracles that Christ could do for others was in relation to the amount of faith they exercised. For instance, the Bible tells us that two blind men followed Jesus begging for mercy upon themselves. Matthew 9:29, 30 declares, "Then touched he their eyes, saying, According to your faith be it unto you. And their eyes were opened."

Matthew 4:23, 24 tells us that "Jesus went about all Galilee, . . . healing all manner of sickness and all manner of disease among the people. And his fame went throughout all Syria; and they brought unto Him all sick people that were taken with divers diseases and torments, and those which were possessed with devils, and those which were lunatick, and those that had the palsy; and he healed them."

On the other hand, people with a low level of faith actually robbed themselves of blessings. Matthew 13:58 reminds us "he did not many mighty works there because of their unbelief." So it is with our prayers for others—we must seek and maintain a high level of faith.

Step 5: Forgiveness makes the difference.

We live in an age where people do not find their prayers answered because they have not first asked God to forgive their own sins. It is my firm practice never to pray for a person unless I raise my heart to God in this way: "Dear heavenly Father, in the name of the Lord Jesus, please forgive me if I have offended Thee in thought, word, or deed. I know, Lord, that Your hand is not shortened that it cannot save, neither Your ear heavy that it cannot hear, but I realize that our iniquities and sins can separate us from Thee and Thy rich blessings [see Isaiah 59:1, 2]. I can't afford to be separated from Thee even for a moment, so please make everything right between Thee and me, I pray."

A large number of Christians mentioned in their letters and phone calls that their prayers seemed to be going nowhere. They asked me what I thought the problem was. First I tried to help by questioning them about their Christian life. But that approach seemed to be a dead end. Finally I asked the Lord to have the Holy Spirit help me to understand the problem.

Before I went to bed that particular night I opened the Bible for something to meditate on before I fell asleep. When I flipped it open I saw the Lord's Prayer. I did not stop there, however, but continued reading. "If ye forgive men their trespasses, your heavenly Father will also forgive you: But if ye forgive not men their trespasses, neither will your Father forgive your trespasses" (Matthew 6:14, 15).

Instantly it occurred to me that the unforgiving attitude of some people could be blocking the way of God's blessings. Since then I have helped many individuals by asking if they have any difficulty in forgiving the shortcomings of others or the wrongs those individuals may have done them.

One woman was puzzled why her prayers seemed so ineffectual. When I brought up this possible attitude, she instantly stated that that was her problem. "In fact," she said, "it's a characteristic that runs in our family. I will always remember my granddad saying, 'If anybody does anything hurtful to you, don't get mad—just wait for the right opportunity, and get even with that person.' " She then admitted that only a miracle of God in her life would enable her to forgive others.

About six months later she called again. But this time rejoicing filled her voice as she told how God had given her the capacity to truly forgive others. And now her prayers were producing beautiful results.

During the past several years I have received letters from around the world telling how the Spirit of God has blessed the lives of both those who have been reading *Incredible Answers to Prayer* and those they have been praying for. Here are some excerpts from those letters. I offer them not to extol myself, but to show what God can do through even the humblest of His servants. God is everywhere looking for channels to pour His blessing and grace on those around us.

A Missionary Couple in Africa

"During the 1990 General Conference session my husband backordered a copy of your book, since the first printing had been sold out. We were disappointed that we couldn't take it back with us then.

"It arrived in January, just at the time when I personally needed the kind of help found in its pages. Through it the Spirit of God brought me inner peace, the type that comes only in the contemplation of the greatness of God, His amazing love that intervenes even in the minutist needs of our lives and sustains our faith so that our 'footsteps slip not' (Psalm 17:5)."

The above two paragraphs have been translated from a three-page letter written in French. My reply brought another letter about two months later.

"Daily our hearts are overflowing with gratitude to God for the victories we are seeing in the lives of those we are praying for," the woman wrote. "The fact that we are seeing such transformations taking place in the lives of many, in itself draws us closer to our Redeemer."

From South America

"Dear Brother Morneau:

"I really don't know how to start, as I have so much to tell you. Let me first praise and thank our heavenly Father for transforming your life . . . And I thank you for having allowed Him to use you in such wonderful ways, and for having written *Incredible Answers to Prayer*, so that the lives of God's people could be encouraged and blessed in these difficult times.

"I have read your wonderful book three times, and am now reading certain portions daily. Every time the Lord teaches me something more wonderful. Your book is helping so many people to learn to pray more effectively, and to see their prayers for others being answered in ways they had not imagined before.

"Many things have arrested my attention as I read your work. One in particular is, God's goodness and faithfulness in honoring those who honor Him. I am amazed at what the Lord can do when a person gives his or her heart to Jesus, and lives to honor Him.

"Permit me to say again, that I have no words to express my gratitude to the Lord and you for such a wonderful book."

The same things will be said of all those who pray for others. God longs for each one of us to open our prayers to Him so that He can use them to bring unending blessing of salvation to this world.

7

Kept From Demon Spirits by the Power of Prayer

We are living in difficult times. In fact, we are moving into that great "time of trouble, such as never was since there was a nation" that the prophet Daniel spoke of (Daniel 12:1). Distress and perplexity plague people of all walks of life. Fear sweeps many as they see only a hopeless future. We are also living in a fast-changing world. Things that just a few years ago seemed impossible, such as the collapse of the Berlin Wall and a redrawing of the map of Europe, are now past history. The dissolution of the former Soviet Union has taken world leaders by surprise.

While the problems of living in today's world occupy people's minds, Satan's angels are redoubling their efforts to "defeat the work of Christ in man's behalf and to fasten souls in [their] snares" (*The Great Controversy*, p. 518).

The devil's main objective is to cause people to lose out on eternal life, and he takes his work most seriously. "To hold the people in darkness and impenitence till the Saviour's mediation is ended, and there is no longer a sacrifice for sin, is the object which he seeks to accomplish" (*ibid.*).

Sad to say, but if the hundreds of letters I have received requesting prayer for loved ones that have lost their way through immorality is any indication, I am forced to conclude that Satan is having huge success.

We are living in unique times, and God is looking to His commandment-keeping people for individuals whom He can use to help conclude His mission on earth. He needs a mighty army of praying people, men and women who understand the rules of engagement in the conflict between good and evil.

God wants those who understand that prayer is not something to persuade a reluctant God to help us here on earth, but rather realize that God and His angels have no legal right in the eyes of the angels and inhabitants of the unfallen worlds to enter Satan's domain unless we as the devil's captives plead the merits of Christ as the reason human beings should be given divine help.

Perhaps an experience I had when I was a spirit worshiper many years ago will illustrate this fact. A satanist priest bragged to me how Satan had forced the Creator to leave the devil's newly acquired domain. The man said that Satan declared that such a demand was his legal right before the universe, and that the devil had gotten his wish.

"At that time," the priest said, "the master [Satan] stated that he and his angels would make themselves invisible to human beings also, thus leaving people free to live their lives as they wanted to. He emphatically argued that the only fair way for supernatural forces to influence human conduct should be by flashing thought images into individual minds."

How much of what the priest said can be believed, I do not know. But much of what the spiritists told me made sense, and actually helped me make a decision for Christ a few months later.

God searches for caring people who are willing to reflect Christ's character. "Love for God, zeal for His glory, and love for fallen humanity, brought Jesus to earth to suffer and die. This was the controlling power in His life. This principle He bids us adopt" (*The Desire of Ages*, p. 330).

Jesus in His human existence on earth demonstrated His great concern for every human being. At times He spent entire nights in prayer for them. What He saw everywhere in the world drove Him to prayer. "The Son of God, looking upon the world, beheld suffering and misery. With pity He saw how men had become victims of satanic cruelty. He looked with compassion upon those who were being corrupted, murdered, and lost" (*ibid.*, p. 36). No wonder He spent every moment praying for the salvation of the human race.

The reasons that compelled Christ to pray for others still exist today, and should prompt us to seek the Holy Spirit's aid in fighting people's spiritual battles against the forces of darkness. After all, as the apostle Paul wrote, "We wrestle not against flesh and blood, but against principalities, against powers, against the rulers of the darkness of this world, against spiritual wickedness in high places" (Ephesians 6:12).

Each one of us is involved in the unceasing struggle between the forces of good and evil. I became acquainted with this conflict after my conversion from spirit worship nearly five decades ago. But through the years I have seen the powers of darkness lose their hold on the lives of great numbers of people as I prayed daily for God to appropriate the merits of Christ's blood to them. He has honored my prayers by having the Holy Spirit continually drive away demonic spirits or protect men and women from their control.

"Earnest, persevering supplication to God in faith . . . can alone avail to bring men the Holy Spirit's aid in the battle against principalities and powers, the rulers of the darkness of this world, and wicked spirits in high places" (*ibid.*, p. 431).

To illustrate how such individuals are "kept by the power of God through faith," I would like to tell you of an experience that took place in 1991. When I get a bundle of letters, I first quickly look them over, then read first the one that most arrests my attention. On June 3 of that year I received one that had the word "Urgent" written on the lower left corner of the envelope. I read it immediately.

"How I would like to talk to you," the writer, a woman I will call Norma White, said. "I'm sure you are swamped with phone calls and letters, as an editorial secretary at the Review and Herald Publishing Association told me when I inquired about your address.

"I'm a dedicated SDA Christian who loves the Lord dearly. A year ago from last January unexpected and strange things began to happen to me, as supernatural forces brought great distress in my life, even to the point of attacking me physically. I couldn't get help from my pastor, as this is a subject that ministers shy away from.

"But when I read your wonderful experiences with intercessory prayer, 'hope sprung eternal' in my heart, and I decided to contact you. If you have time I would very much like to talk to you. My phone number is . . ."

As soon as I finished Mrs. White's letter, I immediately opened my Bible to Matthew's account of the Crucifixion, placed the letter on the open Bible, then implored the Most High that He appropriate the blood of Christ to this victim of satanic cruelty. That evening I phoned her, and she gave me an overview of the situation.

To begin with, she told me that she had been employed by the Seventh-day Adventist denomination for more than 36 years. Her husband had passed away after a three-week illness just a few years before, and she had continued to live in her house alone. I asked her when the demonic spirits had begun to afflict her. She told me part of her story, then completed it in an eight-page letter the next day. I will quote from that letter.

Apparently she had been giving Bible studies to a "gentleman who was much attached to his departed loved ones. As a Christian, I encouraged him to accept Christ as his personal Saviour, to no avail."

From the woman's voice on the phone I could tell that it made Norma uncomfortable to talk about her experiences, but I explained that the only way I could help her was to learn the details of her experience. Thus in her letter she explained that "at night I began hearing windows and doors opening and closing. I would hear footsteps like those of a man going up and down the staircase. Also a dense blackness hovered around me for a time, and for months I suffered harassment and oppression, with a threat that I would die because of my great interest in Henry's [the man she was giving Bible studies to] salvation. . . .

"Without warning I was awakened at 3:00 a.m. one night,

and I felt like I had been tossed up and down on my bed. A dense blackness momentarily hovered around me. Then, shaken violently, I cried out to Jesus to save me. At that very instant the terrible shaking stopped."

Somehow I had the impression that her Bible study person Henry was not the current focus of her problem. When I inquired if she knew of any other reasons the spirits might be bothering her, she told me about a second experience.

"A lady that I know well asked me to fill in for her in taking care of a blind woman two days a week. . . . I had to sleep there, too. This was for five weeks. I felt very uncomfortable during that time. Two days after I finished there, troubles started again, lasting from November till April.

"This time I almost went under, but a dear friend drove 200 miles to take me to her home. One Sunday morning I watched the *Quiet Hour* program. Elder Tucker lovingly spoke of our Lord's sacrifice on Calvary's cross. When I knelt down to thank God for His great love and sacrifice, the terrible shaking started again. Instantly I prayed for Jesus to save me, and the shaking instantly stopped.

"I continued to help out with the blind woman. She had a button on her phone that automatically called me, and I was happy to talk to her and encourage her. Her calls became a daily occurrence.

"At times I felt drained and exhausted after our conversations. Then after a while she became very possessive of me, and it appeared that she was trying to control my life. When the strange blackness began rolling in after I spoke to her, I terminated my association with her."

As Norma would converse with me over the phone, she would comment, "I wonder why Jesus allows the spirits to return." The whole series of experiences puzzled her.

I explained that "Satan is seeking to overcome men today, as he overcame our first parents, by shaking their confidence in their Creator" (*The Great Controversy*, p. 534).

One phenomenon especially disturbed her—the fact that the spirits were beginning to oppress her in church. "While sitting in church, I felt like a tight straitjacket was put on me, and my breath was going to be squeezed out. I immediately went out of the sanctuary and prayed aloud for Jesus to help me." From that time on she naturally felt more and more reluctant to attend church, as the oppression occurred two additional times.

"Why are the evil spirits oppressing me, and not other people?" she asked. "Why would such an experience be taking place in my life? I have always lived for God. And why does Jesus allow the spirits to return? I just can't figure it out."

I concluded that somehow she had been touched by what I would call a taint of evil spirit defilement, that is, something had opened the way for the demonic spirits to have access to her. Had either Henry or the blind woman ever given her anything that she might still have in her possession?

"Yes," she said, thinking a moment, "I have a birthday gift, a Bible, and a couple other items that the blind lady gave me."

I suggested that she dispose of them, as it seems a principle of spirit behavior that they have access to a person if that individual keeps certain objects associated with them in his or her possession. Put them in the garage, I suggested, until she could get rid of them in a more permanent way.

As for her question of why the spirits had selected her to oppress, I told her that quite a few others were having similar experiences, and that such supernatural manifestations would become more and more frequent just before the conflict between good and evil came to an end.

I explained that such supernatural phenomena had been common in the Western world until a couple centuries ago, and still were in other parts of the world. But with the rise of modern science, Satan had decided to convince people that he and his angels did not really exist. Much of the Western world has concluded that the supernatural is simply a figment of the imagination. In this way Satan hopes to make the Bible look like a fairy tale.

About her question of why such things should happen to a person who had lived a God-fearing life, I said as long as we live in this sinful world, none of us have any guarantee that Christ's enemies will not also attack us.

The evil angels kept returning to haunt her because God

allows them the right to approach any person who keeps anything associated with them. Exactly that experience had happened to me. For six months after I accepted Jesus and abandoned spirit worship, they kept rapping on the doors and walls of my small apartment, trying to reestablish contact with me. When I mentioned the problem to my pastor, he asked if I still had anything at my place that had been associated with spirit worship. When I mentioned that I had some books on a closet shelf, he suggested that I dispose of them. After I did, the supernatural harassment ceased.

After going over with Mrs. White what I call my "seven-step recovery program" (material that I give especially to all people who have come into contact with so-called deliverance ministries, and that I will discuss in a coming chapter), I encouraged her to hold on to her faith in the Lord. Since then she has lived in the peace and joy that only the Spirit of God can bring, that same great power that Jesus used during His human ministry to cast out devils (Matthew 12:28). We have kept in touch by letters and telephone calls, and every time I talk to her, I rejoice as I sense her vibrant personality. She tells me again and again that she finds one of her greatest joys in her prayer ministry as she witnesses how God blesses others through it.

Norma is particularly thrilled at seeing marriages once in the process of breaking up now stable and happy. She has become a highly caring person dedicated to the spiritual needs of those she knows. Along with those she prays for, she is being preserved by the power of God bestowed through faith-filled prayer.

A Horrifying Experience

A mother wrote about a daughter named Martha who had been afflicted with mental depression to the point that it had resulted in a nervous breakdown. No sooner had she recovered from that than she began to suffer from various phobias.

Martha became afraid of the dark, afraid of driving a car, afraid of heights that had never bothered her before, and so forth. All of her problems seemed to defy medical science. Medications that had helped others proved useless with her.

Then something unusual happened. During the middle of

the night an unseen presence would wake her up by shaking her bed or doing other strange things. For instance, the shades on her two bedroom windows would suddenly roll to the top of the window case at the same time and with a frightening slam.

The mother realized that demon forces were at work to destroy her daughter. She sought help from Adventist ministers, but they were reluctant to get involved except to say that they would pray for Martha.

Shortly afterward she came into possession of my two books and, having read them, lost no time in getting in contact with me. After I heard the story, I began asking questions that I hoped would lead me to whatever the spirits were using as their avenue to her daughter. Could Martha have been involved in supernatural activities without her realizing it?

The distressed mother said she would get back in touch with me in a day or two after she had had a chance to talk to Martha. Sure enough, the girl mentioned that one of her high school friends had a Ouija board and used it to communicate with the supposed spirit of her dead cousin. The spirit acted friendly to Martha until the girl one day made a comment about her religious upbringing. From then on the spirit refused to answer Martha's requests. Instead it wrote terrible things that it said would happen to the girl.

When I heard the story, I stressed the importance of Martha asking God to forgive her iniquities. God considers conversing with evil spirits through any channel a most dangerous thing to do. I urged for mother and daughter to begin each day with prayer, and for them to request God to appropriate the merits of Christ's shed blood to the girl, and for the Holy Spirit to surround her with an atmosphere of light and peace. Only then would the demonic spirits no longer have access to her. In addition, I sent her my seven-step recovery program.

Soon the Lord of glory gave Martha complete deliverance from her satanic oppression.

CHAPTER

8

A Great Discovery

In a number of letters people have commented how their prayer life has become a most precious experience, and they have achieved a closeness with Christ such as they would never have thought possible in this life. The wording varies, but the theme is the same. They always back up their statements by telling me one or more of their prayer experiences. Here are a few of them.

A man living in a major Canadian city received a copy of *Incredible Answers to Prayer* and was so pleased with what he read that he obtained 50 more copies and gave them to his Catholic relatives and a great number of his friends. Among them was his daughter, who was married to an industrialist. The daughter's husband had been under a doctor's care for some time because of stress-induced burnout.

The high pressure of his job had given him ulcers and at times sent him into fits of uncontrollable anger. His blood pressure had risen dangerously and affected his heart. The man's doctor told the executive's wife that he would not live long unless he made some drastic changes in his life.

The news saddened the woman until she remembered a statement that she had read on page 84 of *Incredible Answers* just a few days before. There I had said that the Lord Jesus is an "expert in salvation, specializing in hopeless cases." She understood the statement also to mean that the Lord was a problem solver of the highest magnitude, and that if she interceded for her husband, He would remove his many burdens and heal the man.

With her Bible in one hand and *Incredible Answers to Prayer* in the other, she began praying for her husband with a faith that brought almost instant results. Within two weeks she saw noticeable changes taking place. Two weeks later the man went to the doctor. There tests indicated that his condition had made a striking improvement.

Soon I received an enthusiastic letter from her requesting my phone number. (Early in 1985 my cardiologist had insisted that I have an unlisted phone number so I would get all the rest I needed.) When she called me, she said, "I just knew that you would have a French accent. Oh, how glad I am to be able to talk to you."

After we had chatted a bit, she told how she had attended a Billy Graham evangelistic crusade in her city a few years previously. Christ had become very real to her at the time. Somehow the mysticism that had enshrouded her concept of Jesus vanished, and she grasped the reality of His being "the way, the truth, and the life," her only means of salvation.

She realized, contrary to what she had been brought up to believe, that she had to abandon any idea of any other intercessor and yield her life directly and entirely to Jesus. He alone had died on Calvary for our salvation, and to Him alone should she commit her life.

"As wonderful as those years of living for Christ have been," she said, "your book has opened up a whole new understanding of His ministration as our great high priest in the Holy of Holies in the heavenly sanctuary. It is adding to my Christian experience a wealth of heavenly grace. Interceding for others has brought unlimited joy into my life as well as wonderful blessings into the lives of others."

Despite the fact that she was calling during daytime rates, she spent more than two hours talking to me. She had many questions about my religious beliefs, and my conversion to the Seventh-day Adventist Church seemed to fascinate her.

Her husband's condition continued to improve. The last time she talked to me she had an interesting story to tell. Although the man was not a churchgoing person, he had no objections to her and her children practicing their religious faith. One day she was writing a letter to a woman friend when she suddenly remembered that she had an appointment with a beautician, dropped everything, and rushed out.

Sometime later the husband came home. Seeing the unfinished letter on the desk, and being curious by nature, he began to read it. It told how his wife had been praying for him and how his health had dramatically improved. He did not say a word about what he had discovered until one day he had a new Cadillac delivered to his surprised wife at their residence. When she asked why he was giving her such a marvelous present, he inquired, "Where did you learn to pray such power-filled prayers—prayers that produce such amazing results?"

"I have made some wonderful discoveries," she answered. Then she told him the whole story.

Motivated to Write

It is always interesting to look at the postmarks on the letters I receive. In fact, Hilda always tells me where they are from before handing them to me. But nothing exceeds the joy of reading the messages they contain.

As I write this it is two days before Thanksgiving Day. We will be celebrating it with our daughter and son-in-law, Linda and Mike Hatley, here in California. As we gather around the dinner table, we will be thanking the Lord for many things. One of them will be the large volume of letters that have given me the opportunity to hear of the wonderful ways in which God's Spirit is blessing the lives of others. Here is an example.

"Dear Mr. Morneau:

"It is in appreciation of blessings received that I am motivated to write this letter to say thank you for having written your book. . . .

"I joined God's remnant church 23 years ago, and I can say without exaggeration that those have been wonderful years. But now that I have read your book on prayer, I can see that the future holds greater joys in the Lord, as I am now witnessing many of my prayers for others being answered in remarkable ways.

"You see, I have made a wonderful discovery in reading your book. I now see how the Holy Spirit is able to make our prayers become reality."

Emphasizing how he now realized that the Holy Spirit is "the divine power which is necessary for the growth and prosperity of the church" (*The Acts of the Apostles*, p. 50), he thanked me for allowing God to use me to revitalize his Christian experience. Then he told me what has been happening in the lives of people who had lost interest in the church, and for whom he had been praying. "When I saw a couple walk into our church who had not been there for 12 years, I became very excited about my prayer results."

A Stabilizing Force

It is especially interesting to hear from busy people because I realize what a great effort had to be put forth to put such a letter in the mail. I once was in that position, always looking for a few moments to do some personal thing.

"I have planned on writing to you for a long time," one such letter began, "but haven't been able to do so until now. My busy schedule imposes itself upon me in such a way that it deprives me of the opportunity to do a number of other things that I also consider important, such as writing to you.

"I am in the medical field, and my occupation is very demanding.

"Your book has come into my life just at the time that I needed very special help from the Lord. I believe it to be an answer to my prayers. I have been a Seventh-day Adventist for many years, and consider myself well read in the area of spiritual matters. But as I read your book I discovered a number of things that are now making a world of difference in my Christian walk.

"My prayer life has become a joyous and stabilizing force in the way I live, and is producing precious results in the lives of those I have been praying for."

Letters that arrive in business-size envelopes usually

indicate a major message or problem. As a result, I read them first. Here is an example.

"There are many wonderful things I want to tell you, but I really don't know where to start. Our family is so perfectly happy now because of how God has blessed in so many ways.

"Recently our hearts overflowed with joy as our dad was baptized into God's remnant church. For more than 40 years Mother and the rest of us children had been praying that our father would come to the Lord. But tobacco had a powerful hold on his life, and spiritual things did not have any attraction for him. Besides, his business activities kept him too busy to take time for God.

"One day in 1991 Mother bought a copy of your book at the Adventist Book Center, and as she read it, all kinds of thoughts entered her mind on how we could pray for Dad in the positive and time-proven ways that you mentioned.

"My sister and I read the book in its entirety also, and made some wonderful discoveries. I don't know if 'discover' is the right word to use here, because we naturally already knew about prayer, but never in the positive way in which you have explained it.

"Reading the prayer experiences and how you presented people's needs before the Lord helped us a lot. We began to pray more meaningful prayers, and having asked for the Holy Spirit to help us pray more power-filled prayers, we became aware that the merits of the precious blood Christ shed on Calvary was indeed the key that opens the way to salvation.

"Mr. Morneau, we thank you so much for having helped us see how the Holy Spirit is able to reach and save the 'unsavable.'

"We went on praying on a daily basis that the Holy Spirit would surround our dad with a precious atmosphere of light and peace, and in so doing, block off the perplexing and distressing suggestions from demonic spirits that were causing him to carry such heavy burdens.

"Some time went by; then we began to see an encouraging change in him. He began to smile more often. After a while he became more talkative—to the extent that he would tell

Mother a lot about what was taking place at his business, something he had never done before.

"One day he said to her, 'Mary [not her real name], I believe that as you are getting older, you are getting better at praying.'

"Mom almost toppled over, she was so shocked. He continued by saying that some time ago he had been having a terrible time getting the right type of merchandise shipped to him because of some bad mix-up at the factory. Then he explained how he had solved the problem.

" 'I believe that you are getting better at praying because of this,' he told Mom. 'I was going to phone the top manager and give him a piece of my mind. But the strangest thing happened. Instead of building up anger as I do when I get furious over a problem, I just remained calm. I couldn't seem to get mad. It surprised the life out of me.

" 'Then I thought of you, and how you solve problems by praying. The thought entered my mind that you were undoubtedly praying for me to get over that terrible habit of mine. It was a powerful impression. Strange, isn't it? It's hard for me to tell you this, but I know that I should.

" 'As a result I asked the Lord if He would be kind enough to please solve the mix-up at the factory even though I had never given Him much of my time. I added that you knew Him well, and maybe He could take that into consideration and help me. And sure enough, an hour later I received a phone call from the factory assuring me of overnight delivery.' "

As I read the woman's letter, my heart thrilled with happiness as I saw how wonderfully God's Spirit worked to lead that man to Christ.

"Mother, my sister, and I kept praying," the woman explained in her letter, "but we did not dare talk religion with him, especially after the way he had reacted when Mother had joined the Adventist Church 40 years before. And in a way we felt good about not doing so, because we knew the Holy Spirit was ministering to him. Our father was in good hands. 'What better help could he get?' Mother would say. Besides, if he wanted to know anything about religious matters, Mother had a whole bookcase full of good books.

"One day he announced that he was no longer smoking. We congratulated him for his determination to overcome such a powerful and destructive force in his life, and got real excited when we realized that our prayers were being answered so marvelously.

"As he was retiring one evening, he pointed to *Incredible Answers to Prayer* on Mom's night table and said, 'How do you like that book on prayer you have been reading? Are those prayer answers really as incredible as the cover claims? Could I look at it?'

"Mother was both shocked at his questions and at the same time exceedingly joyful in the Lord for Dad's new interest in spiritual things. He read two chapters of the book, turned off the light, and went to sleep. The following night he read the same two chapters, then went to sleep. On the third night he read chapter 2, commented on it being a fascinating work, then again went to sleep. For the next two nights he read the same chapter, but did not say a word about it.

"Mother was eager to hear his opinion of what he had read, but dared not ask him a question. She kept reminding herself, 'I must not try to do the work of the Holy Spirit.' Dad later told us that he was especially fascinated with the discussion of distrust of God and unbelief on pages 26-28 of that chapter.

"On the following Sabbath he informed Mother that he would no longer go to his place of business on Saturdays. Instead he would stay home. Delighted, Mom thought of inviting him to go to church with her, then said within herself, 'I better not. The decision has to come from him.'

"Then she had a big surprise awaiting her when she returned home.

"'Well, Mary,' said Dad, 'I have something very important to tell you. While you were at church, I read the remainder of *Incredible Answers to Prayer*. I have also talked to the Lord about all that I have read, and He has impressed me greatly that the time has come to "stand in holy time," as the author mentioned on page 28 of the book. Next Sabbath I will go to church with you. We'll have to get up a little earlier because I move very slowly on Saturdays. Oh, you may tell our daughters about my new decision, as it may make them happy.'

"Mr. Morneau, I hope I haven't tired you with my long letter. I only thought of telling you of our prayer experience with Dad—in all its details—because it is such a wonderful example of how God's Holy Spirit can transform lives, even in individuals whose cases appear hopeless. Think of it! Forty years of waiting for a miracle to take place in a person's life is surely a long span of time.

"I thank the Lord every day for your book, and you will always be remembered in my prayers. My mother thanks you, my sister thanks you, and I thank you with all my heart for having written about your prayer experiences.

"In Christian love, . . ."

CHAPTER

9

Unconditional Love

Since my book on intercessory prayer came off the press, I have had a number of experiences that not only challenged my human limitations, but at times have even proved embarrassing to me.

Some individuals have gotten the idea that I possess a superior intellect and understanding that can solve any problem, whether religious or secular. They think I have some kind of Solomonic wisdom. At other times they have considered me to be their spiritual leader, and have actually told me so. Permit me to illustrate.

A woman from the country of Ecuador, visiting relatives in the United States, obtained my address from the publisher and wrote to ask for my telephone number. "It's important," she said, so I sent it to her.

A few days later she called me, and after we had conversed for a few minutes, she referred to me as "Pastor Morneau." At first I thought nothing of it, but when she repeated the title several more times, I mentioned that I was not an ordained minister, just an ordinary layman. She thanked me for telling her and continued talking.

Several minutes passed, then she said, "Pastor Morneau, would you do me a favor?"

"If it's within my capacity to do so, and if you will stop

calling me 'Pastor Morneau,' I would be glad to."

Pausing for three or four seconds, she said, "It is very difficult for me to think that you are not a minister of God. I have received so much help, encouragement in the Lord, and outright peace and contentment from reading your book that I consider you my minister." Then in a voice that reflected both submission and a longing for approval, she added, "Would it be agreeable with you if I continue thinking of you as my pastor? My number one spiritual leader? It would make me so happy."

I gave her the same answer I did my wife when she wanted to get a cat: "I guess it's OK, if it makes you happy." (I am allergic to cats.)

Whenever a person begins expressing esteem for me, I immediately direct his or her attention to Christ, who has blessed my life in so many ways. All glory must be given to the Holy Trinity, I tell them. All honor should go to the Father, Son, and Holy Spirit. Whatever I have accomplished through my prayers or writings has been because of their power and divine love.

Besides religious counsel, many seek more secular advice. One topic that keeps coming up is what parents of adult children who have left God and the church should do about the inheritance that they would normally receive. Should they drop the children from their wills? Should they teach them a lesson by not leaving them anything?

Some of the parents who contacted me had already decided to remove their children from their wills, but wanted to see what I thought of the matter. In every case I tried to use all the tact I could muster. I prayed that I would say the right thing and not offend them.

More recently I had an experience that will perhaps solve this great problem for a lot of people. A wealthy widow in her late 70s contacted me and announced that she intended to disinherit her two middle-aged children who had no use for God. As I had done previously, I suggested that she pray about it. Surely, I said, the Lord would guide her in doing what was right in her situation.

"As I read your book," she replied, "I noticed that when you faced a problem, you immediately asked the Lord, 'What should I do?' Almost instantly a verse of Scripture or a passage from Ellen White would come to mind—a verse or passage that would contain the right answer. I would greatly appreciate your doing the same kind of praying for my problem."

That night as I conversed in prayer with my heavenly Father, thanking Him for the wonderful ways in which His Holy Spirit had given me guidance in the past, I presented the woman's request. I asked for special enlightenment, special insight that would guide Christian parents faced with the question of disinheriting their children.

It is my custom when praying to pause and meditate every so often upon the subject I am presenting. I may ask the Lord to impress on my mind the right thing to say or do. And quite often a verse of the Bible will come to mind that will remove all uncertainty and open a clear path before me.

On that particular night the words "unconditional love" popped into my mind. As I repeated them a few times, trying to figure out how they would relate to the problem in question, a verse from the fifteenth chapter of Luke flooded my thoughts: "And the son said unto him, Father, I have sinned against heaven, and in thy sight, and am no more worthy to be called thy son" (verse 21).

Years before I had memorized the parable of the prodigal son to remind myself of God's goodness toward fallen human beings. In addition, I vividly remembered the prodigal son experience a couple friends had suffered through.

The couple had told us how their son, having just graduated from high school, broke their hearts one day when he decided to leave home and never come back. Although these parents had no money to send their son on his way, the other parallels were there: the unexpected news of his leaving, jealousy from his belief that his parents had treated his sister better, etc.

Before he left, the son vented his bitterness on his parents. The mother's heart broke and wouldn't heal. She cried every day for at least two months, until she came to grips with the fact that we live in cruel world and that she was only one of countless mothers suffering from such tragic rejection.

As the father pondered the whole experience in his aching heart, he did the best he could to comfort his wife. A couple years passed by without any news from the son; then one day the parents received a call from the sheriff of Erie County, New York, telling them that the boy was in jail. He had become involved in a burglary ring.

Sad as the occasion was, they rejoiced over the fact that at least he was still alive. Losing no time in going to see him, they also arranged for an attorney to get the son released.

Afterward, a number of the couples' friends observed that if he had been their son, they would have let the young man stay in jail until he "rotted." But the parents still loved their son. They stood by him through the long ordeal of the courts, and in the end, they picked up the tab for the legal and other costs.

That incident flashed through my mind. I instantly recognized it as an illustration of unconditional love in action. The type of love that comes directly from the heart of God.

Turning the light on, I took my Bible and read the parable again. I determined to comprehend God's unconditional love and how it seeks to help us form a character like His. Jesus said, "Be ye therefore perfect, even as your Father which is in heaven is perfect" (Matthew 5:48). The father in the parable reflects our heavenly Father.

Longing for the young man's return, he probably glanced down the road several times a day, hoping to see him silhouetted against the horizon. When the son did come back, the Bible says that "when he was yet a great way off, his father saw him, and had compassion, and *ran*, and fell on his neck, and kissed him" (Luke 15:20).

I am inclined to believe that the son was not only in rags, but also smelled like the pigs he had been tending. In *Christ's Object Lessons* we read, "The father will permit no contemptuous eye to mock at his son's misery and tatters. He takes from his own shoulders the broad, rich mantle, and wraps it around the son's wasted form" (pp. 203, 204).

Here we see unconditional love exemplified. But what if the father had met his son on normal human terms?

Imagine the father going out to meet his son, not to welcome him home, but to even the score. When the young man gets within about 25 feet, the father commands him to stop and approach no closer. "Son," he says, "you smell terrible, and you are in rags. What in the world have you done with all that money I gave you? Besides, why are you coming home? Who gave you the impression that you would ever be welcome here?"

The boy tries to explain, but every time he starts to say something his father cuts him off. Then his dad gives the boy a piece of his mind.

"I told you when you left home never to come back unless you intended to be a model person. And I get the distinct impression that you haven't learned a single thing that will make you a better person."

The young man puts his hand up several times, trying to indicate that he wants to say something in response, but his father won't give him a chance. "What do you have to say that is so important that you keep trying to interrupt me?" the father finally barks.

"Dad, I haven't eaten in three days. Do you think that we could go home, and while I have something to eat, you could lay down the rules that I will now have to live by?"

"You haven't eaten in three days? Well, it serves you right. You deserve not to eat after having wasted all the money I gave you."

I thought long and carefully about that parable. When the wealthy widow called again, I told her how I had prayed about whether she should disinherit her grown children. But before I told her what I had thought about, I asked her a question. "How interested are you in seeing them in the earth made new?"

"Why do you ask me such a question?" she replied. "I would do anything to see John and Mary in God's kingdom."

Then I suggested that if she was unable to lead them back to Christ while she was still alive, she could—with the help of the Holy Spirit—still make a powerful impact upon their lives after she died by manifesting her unconditional love for them in a special way.

"You could write and seal a letter," I suggested, "with instructions for it not to be opened until after your death. It should accompany your will, and could be left with your attorney. Its message should be one that will set forth before them your unfailing love for them.

"Perhaps you could begin by telling of the joy and happiness they brought into your home from the day they were born. How you and your husband were enriched by the things they did. How they smiled when you talked to them, their excitement over some special toy, their inquisitiveness when they began to walk, etc.

"The more cheerfully you describe the events in their lives that made you happy, the better they will understand how devoted you were to their happiness and well-being both in this life and for eternity. With the Spirit of God speaking to their lives at the time of your departure, they could be led to reevaluate the way they live. Perhaps recognizing the uncertain span of this life, they might adopt new values and start living for those things that lead to life eternal. Then they might seek the privilege of being with you in the earth made new."

The woman began to cry and had to pause to regain her composure. Finally she said, "Mr. Morneau, I am so glad that I talked to you. A good friend had advised me to disinherit my children as the best way of teaching them a lesson they would never forget.

"But now I realize that it would only have hardened their hearts. Then they would never have followed the example I have given them in serving the Lord. To have walked the earth made new with me—that would have been the last thing they would have wanted to do."

Since then I have had the occasion to help two other persons with the same problem. In each case I have set forth before them God's unconditional love and its contrast to ordinary human love and asked them how they would demonstrate such love in their particular situation.

10

Your Thoughts—Are They Your Own?

We live in a fast-paced world and face constant pressure from every direction. Powerful influences clamor for our attention, and we often have to make important decisions on the run.

Fast food, computerized banking, cellular phones that let us talk while hurtling down a superhighway, and jumbo jets that transport us across a continent in hours—everything seems designed to propel us through life at high velocity. But such a life is taxing many to the breaking point. A growing number of the letters I receive tell of increasing need for divine power just to cope with today's rocketing world. People cry out for more strength and endurance. Consider these excerpts.

Desperate

"I do not want to be a burden to you, but I am desperate to get divine help to keep me from losing my mind. Although I am a total stranger, I am writing hoping that you will understand my great need, and will intercede before God in my behalf . . ."

Failing

"I would appreciate your praying for me, because my mind is really failing me. I have a problem with depression. . . . My faith is weak, and my mind is very negative.

"You are right when you say in your book that negative thoughts are disastrous. I have learned that by experience, yet I can't help myself. I just can't keep my mind on the bright side of things. Although I have had counseling and been prescribed medication and other helps, they have not solved my problem.

"I fear that if this condition continues much longer, I might have to be placed in an insane asylum. . . . Would you please pray for me, and if Jesus impresses you with some guidance for my problem, would you please write?"

Afflicted

"I am writing with the hope that perhaps you would be willing to pray for me. I have been afflicted with disabling depression for quite a long time, making it impossible in some instances to reason or think straight. Although I have been under medical care, doctors have not been able to help much.

"I told my last doctor that it seems at times as if some power has a hold upon me that I cannot throw off. He suggested that I talk to my minister about my problems, as I could be oppressed by the powers of darkness. Do you think such a thing could be taking place in my life? I am a God-loving person, and have been an SDA all my life."

Great Pain

". . . I can't cope with all of this. I am in great pain, mental anguish, and depression. . . . I am asking God to put me to sleep."

No Way to Cope

"All my grown children have left the church because they are not finding the help they need to cope with life in this day and age. Their minds are being distressed and perplexed to the point that their marriages are breaking up, and we grandparents are faced with bringing up some of the little ones if we don't want them to live in misery. . . . There is something strange about it all. Brother Morneau, we need your prayers desperately."

The letters from which I have taken these excerpts are not the worst ones I have received. Some tell how the writer plans to kill himself or herself. Others describe unbelievable suffering and agony. People reveal to me things they would not disclose even to their pastors. They describe a world in which unseen forces are at work whose sole purpose is to sow human misery and destruction. The deplorable thing is that few have any sense of the power or activity of such forces and how they can oppress the unguarded human mind.

During my days as a spirit worshiper, a spiritist priest once commented that demonic spirits can wear out our life forces by overstimulating our imaginations. He said that they have the ability to flash images into the mind so subtly that people believe that they are their own thoughts. They love to confuse the human mind, he bragged. "Since people believe that all thoughts are their own," he said, "they are appalled by what they find in their minds. They think that is what they must really be like. The spirits use that revulsion to depress people to the point that they begin to hate themselves. If such thoughts can possibly enter their minds, human beings reason, then they must be horrible people.

"On the other hand, the spirits lead some to think they have superior intellect because of what they suggest to their minds. Such individuals begin to criticize others less endowed, and feel that it is their duty to tell them how to live. Their words poison and alienate."

We hear a lot today about people experiencing "mood swings." They can be talking and laughing one moment, then for no apparent reason turn irritable or even want to start a fight. Sometimes the cause is physical or psychological problems, but other times they can be succumbing to what I call satanic suggestions. In ways that we do not yet understand, Satan and his spirits can influence a person's mental state in disastrous ways. It's much easier to pray for an individual caught up in such mood swings when we realize that we are seeking divine protection for him or her from evil influences. Our prayer in such cases become part of the "ministry of reconciliation" that the apostle Paul speaks of.

The first volume of *Testimonies for the Church* contains a short article entitled "Sympathy at Home." Ellen White writes of a couple referred to as Brother and Sister C, who were experiencing many difficulties. She saw in vision that much of their problem had its origin in satanic influence on the man's thoughts.

"You have a diseased imagination and deserve pity," she told him. "Yet no one can help you as well as yourself. If you want faith, talk faith; talk hopefully. . . . If you suffer Satan to control your thoughts as you have done, you will become a special subject for him to use and will ruin your own soul and the happiness of your family" (p. 699).

Addressing the wife, Mrs. White said, "Brother C deserves pity. He has so long felt unhappy that life has become a burden to him. . . . His imagination is diseased, and he has so long kept his eyes on the dark picture that if he meets with adversity or disappointment, he imagines that everything is going to ruin. . . . The more he thinks this, the more miserable he makes his life and the lives of all around him. He has no reason to feel as he does; it is all the work of Satan" (p. 703).

When I say that we can fall under the influence of satanic suggestions, that does not mean that we are demon-possessed, as too often claimed by those involved in deliverance ministries (see chapter 11). When Jesus began telling His disciples that He would die and be resurrected again, the disciple Peter rebuked Him (Matthew 16:21, 22). Jesus responded to Peter's rebuke by declaring to the disciple, "Get thee behind me, Satan: thou art an offence unto me: for thou savourest not the things that be of God, but those that be of men" (verse 23).

Although Jesus attributed the disciple's action as originating from Satan, He did not mean that Peter was demon-possessed, but merely that the man had let himself fall under satanic influence. There is a clear difference.

When I reply to those who have written the kinds of letters I excerpted at the beginning of this chapter, I make a special effort to encourage them, directing their attention to the fact that "the weapons of our warfare are not carnal, but mighty through God to the pulling down of strong holds; casting down imaginations, and every high thing that exalteth itself against the knowledge of God, and bringing into captivity every thought to the obedience of Christ" (2 Corinthians 10:4, 5).

I especially stress the importance of praying for the Holy Spirit to fight their spiritual battles for them. "Earnest, persevering supplications to God in faith . . . can alone avail to bring men the Holy Spirit's aid in the battle against principalities and powers, the rulers of the darkness of this world, and wicked spirits in high places" (*The Desire of Ages*, p. 431).

Many of those who have turned to prayer with a full understanding of what they were up against are now enjoying glorious victories over what had once been crushing problems.

We must take seriously Satan's attacks on believers. Ellen White writes that "there is little enmity against Satan and his works, because there is so great ignorance concerning his power and malice, and the vast extent of his warfare against Christ and His church. Multitudes are deluded here. They do not know that their enemy is a mighty general who controls the minds of evil angels, and that with well-matured plans and skillful movements he is warring against Christ to prevent the salvation of souls.

"Among professed Christians, and even among ministers of the gospel, there is hardly a reference to Satan. . . . While men are ignorant of his devices, this vigilant foe is upon their track every moment. He is intruding his presence in every department of the household, in every street of our cities, in the churches, in the national councils, in the courts of justice, perplexing, deceiving, seducing, everywhere ruining the souls and bodies of men, women, and children, breaking up families, sowing hatred, emulation, strife, sedition, murder. And the Christian world seems to regard these things as though God had appointed them and they must exist" (*The Great Controversy*, pp. 507, 508).

While the servant of the Lord set forth the immensity of Satan's activities against the human family, she also gave us words of encouragement in our struggle against him. "The power and malice of Satan and his host might justly alarm us were it not that we may find shelter and deliverance in the *superior power* of the Redeemer. We carefully secure our homes with bolts and locks to protect our property and our lives from evil men; but we seldom think of the evil angels who are constantly seeking access to us, and against whose attacks we have, in our own strength, no method of defense.

"If permitted, they can distract our minds, disorder and torment our bodies, destroy our possessions and our lives. Their only delight is in misery and destruction. . . . *But those who follow Christ are ever safe under His watchcare. Angels that excel in strength are sent from heaven to protect them. The wicked one cannot break through the guard which God has stationed about His people*" (*ibid.*, p. 517; italics supplied).

The Lord has given us beautiful minds, and blessed us with the capacity to form images in our minds of things not present to the senses. God has endowed us with the ability to create new ideas or to combine old ones in new ways. That crowning element is our imagination. Let us always watch and pray over it with all possible diligence so that the enemies of our Lord will not do it any injury. Only through divine help can those tragic men and women who write to me overcome the terrible discouragement and misery that Satan and this sin-filled world heaps upon them.

CHAPTER

11

Deliverance Ministries

One of the most frequent questions I receive is for my opinion of the so-called deliverance ministries. Many of the writers have had relatives who have become involved with such organizations. Individuals belonging to deliverance ministries have convinced the loved ones that they were demon-possessed, and whether they actually were before, now the relatives find themselves continually harassed by demonic spirits. Because I have seen so much grief and injury, I feel that I must respond to these letters.

To begin with, I will recount the experience of a Christian woman by the name of Doherty, whose daughter Clara requested exorcism after listening to a sermon by someone active in deliverance ministries. The daughter became convinced from the sermon that she too was demon-possessed.

As Mrs. Doherty told me over the phone, the sermon totally ruined Clara's faith in Christ, and her life has been nothing but misery ever since. She hears voices almost continually, and they wake her up some nights, refusing to let her sleep until the early hours of the morning. One exorcist minister even told the daughter that she had better get used to hearing the voices of demons because they would be with her forever.

Mrs. Doherty had obtained a copy of *Incredible Answers to Prayer* and read it in her bedroom one night without her daughter's knowledge. Then she prayed that God would help her be able to write me about Clara's problem. A short while later the daughter bounced out of her bedroom in great distress and said, "Mother, who is Roger Morneau?"

Mrs. Doherty asked why she wanted to know. The girl replied that a voice had warned her, "Don't let your mother phone Roger Morneau. We hate him with a passion, and besides, he can't help you anyway. If your mother phones him, we won't let you sleep for days."

According to Mrs. Doherty, when her daughter commands in the name of Jesus for the spirits to leave her, they laugh and say that there is no way she can make them go away. The problem soon reached the point where the girl was thinking of killing herself to stop the demonic oppression.

"Some individuals have taken upon themselves to do the work of the Holy Spirit," I wrote back to Mrs. Doherty, "and a harvest of misery has been produced. As a result, a great many Christians have become victims of satanic cruelty.

"My own experience of having been at one time a spiritist has helped me to understand the dangers of what your daughter has become involved in. It has unmasked to me the nature of the power that propels these so-called deliverance ministries.

"First, let me draw your attention to the fact that some of those who will find themselves among the wicked below the walls of the New Jerusalem will have had active careers of casting demons out of people. Listen to the words of Jesus:

" 'Many will say to me in that day, Lord, Lord, have we not prophesied in thy name? and in thy name have cast out devils? . . . Then I will profess unto them, I never knew you: depart from me, ye that work iniquity' [Matthew 7:22, 23].

"I understand Jesus to mean here that some of those who appear to cast demons out of people are not really doing the work of Christ, but of the devil. Many wonder how such a thing could be. But when you focus on them the light of the Word of God, as well as the lesser light, the writings of the Spirit of Prophecy, you will recognize that these self-proclaimed exorcists have been taken in by a powerful deception.

"Deuteronomy 18:10-12 gives a list of nine activities that will bring people into contact with the supernatural. Moses declared being involved in these activities especially disturbs God because He knows how dangerous they are.

"Verse 10: 'There shall not be found among you any one that maketh his son or his daughter to pass through the fire, or that useth divination, or an observer of times, or an enchanter, or a witch.'

"Verse 11: 'Or a charmer, or *a consulter with familiar spirits,* or a wizard, or a necromancer.'

"Verse 12: 'For all that do these things are an abomination unto the Lord: and because of these abominations the Lord thy God doth drive them out from before thee.'

"The surrounding nations performed such occult practices, and God forbade the Israelites to have anything to do with them. I would like to bring your attention back to verse 11 and the phrase 'a consulter with familiar spirits.'

During my affiliation with demon worshipers I was amazed to discover that they classified spirits into three distinct groups. The 'friendly' spirits were those who specialized in deceiving people. Lying spirits, they love to appear as the supposed spirits of the dead.

"The other two groups they named were the 'warriors' and the 'oppressors.' The 'warriors,' they said, concentrate on causing discord in families, hatred among classes of society, and outright wars among nations. The last group, the 'oppressors,' find their greatest delight in inflicting misery and destruction on people.

"Now let us see how long a minister of the gospel conversing with a 'friendly' spirit would have remained alive among the people of Israel. Leviticus 20:26, 27 tells us, 'Ye shall be holy unto me: for I the Lord am holy. . . . A man also or woman that hath a familiar spirit, or that is a wizard, shall surely be put to death: they shall stone them with stones: their blood shall be upon them.'

"The gospel ministers who have been conversing with demonic spirits through possessed individuals should count themselves fortunate that they did not live during Bible times. If they had, their careers would have been short ones.

" 'Satan is seeking to overcome men today, as he overcame our first parents, by shaking their confidence in their Creator' (*The Great Controversy*, p. 534). Satan's most effective way of undermining people's confidence in God is through spiritual leaders.

"For example, when a minister of the gospel tells a person that he or she is possessed with a demon of fear (or any other 'kind' of demon), he has in essence told that person that she will spend the rest of his or her life in a spiritual prison.

"Instantly one of Satan's demons brings the thought to mind that Jesus has failed the person completely. That He, in whom he or she had placed complete trust to save, has not been able to protect him or her from demon possession. As happened to your daughter, such a thought shatters confidence in Christ. Now the way is wide open for a demonic spirit to move in and possess, taking complete control of the faculties.

"Let me assure you, however, that all is not lost with your daughter. Here is a seven-step recovery program that I have given to a number of persons victimized by the so-called deliverance ministries.

"1. Throw out or destroy all literature that exalts deliverance ministries. Demonic spirits have a right to stay with all objects that bear their taint of defilement.

"2. Do not speak to demonic spirits even to command them to depart in the name of Jesus. Let the Holy Spirit do that work. Even Jesus said that He depended on the Spirit of God to cast out demons [Matthew 12:28].

"3. Early every morning read the account of Christ's crucifixion found in Matthew 27:24-54. It only takes about four minutes to read, and will greatly bless your life.

"4. Ask God for forgiveness of sin whether it be in thoughts, words, or deeds.

"5. Plead the merits of the blood that Christ shed at Calvary as the reason the Holy Spirit should fight your spiritual battles. 'Earnest, persevering supplication to God in faith . . .

can alone avail to bring men the Holy Spirit's aid in the battle against principalities and powers, the rulers of the darkness of this world, and wicked spirits in high places' [*The Desire of Ages*, p. 431].

"6. Pray for God to restore the faith that you once had in Christ's power to save so that you will once again have an unfaltering trust in our great Redeemer.

"7. Memorize the Word of God in order to live a victorious, successful Christian life. Fill your mind with passages of Scripture that will give you hope, encouragement, and joy in the Lord.

"I know from personal experience how the above steps can help us escape the harassment of demonic spirits."

In my letter to Mrs. Doherty I also gave additional details about her personal needs as an intercessor in behalf of her daughter, and how to lift Christ in all His glory before Clara so that the girl could regain her faith in Him.

Besides God's express command not to converse with spirits, there is still another reason we should avoid dealings with deliverance ministries. To rebuke spirits as such people do is to take onto oneself a divine attribute. Those who practice deliverance ministries are actually putting themselves in the role of God Himself. Only God has the right or power to rebuke demons.

Let me explain by sharing with you a few passages of Scripture. If you go to a concordance and look up the use of the word "rebuke" in the Old Testament, you will notice an interesting thing: God is the one who does the rebuking. Often He rebukes the sea, an Old Testament symbol of the evil or anything else that opposes God (some examples include Psalm 18:15; Psalm 104:5-7; Psalm 106:9; Exodus 15:4-10; Isaiah 50:2; and Nahum 1:3, 4).

God continues to rebuke the sea even in the New Testament, as we see in Matthew 8:23-27. After Jesus rebuked the stormy Sea of Galilee (verse 26), they exclaim to each other, "What manner of man is this, that even the winds and the sea obey him!" (verse 27). Because they were steeped in Scripture, they sensed that Jesus had done something that only the Lord

God Himself could and had the right to do.

But besides rebuking the sea as a symbol of evil, God in the Bible rebukes something else: Satan and those forces the devil employs against God and His people (Zechariah 3:1, 2; Psalm 76:9; Isaiah 17:13). A careful study of those passages in which the Bible shows God rebuking something shows that He alone has the authority and power to deal with those forces that try to block His will, especially on the supernatural level.

Mark 9:14-29 tells how Jesus heals a boy after rebuking the demon that possessed the child. Although Jesus, being fully God like the Father, could have employed His divine authority to cast such a demon out, here in His human nature He links it with intercessory prayer (verse 29). In His perfect humanness He called upon the Holy Spirit to drive the demon out.

Jesus also rebukes demons in Mark 1:21-28, and in Mark 8:33 He specifically rebukes Satan as the instigator of Peter's rebuke (verse 32). Jesus casts out demons in Matthew 8:28-34. Although He does not use the verb "rebuke," the incident does immediately follow His rebuke of the storm on the sea.

What does this mean? Jesus has the right to rebuke demons and the forces of evil. It is His divine attribute. The disciples cast out demons because Jesus had commissioned them to do so for a time. But to take the attribute upon ourselves is to put ourselves in the place of God. Adam and Eve sought to have attributes of God, and He had to cast them out of the Garden of Eden. Deliverance ministries are also trying to put themselves into the role of God, and that can lead only to confusion and destruction. When anyone tries to take God's responsibility of casting out demons, they are committing Adam and Eve's sin again. Naturally Satan and his agents rejoice when we attempt to exorcise evil spirits, because we are playing into demonic hands.

The Lord of glory who at creation could speak and "it was so" has the power to protect us from all evil spirits. We need never fear their power or threat when we remember that Jesus has given us His word: "I will never leave thee, nor forsake thee" (Hebrews 13:5). Paul triumphantly declared, "For I am persuaded, that neither death, nor life, nor angels, nor principalities, nor powers, nor things present, nor things to come, nor height, nor depth, nor any other creature, shall be able to separate us from the love of God, which is in Christ Jesus our Lord" (Romans 8:38, 39).

Jesus claims the capacity "to present you faultless before the presence of his glory with exceeding joy, to the only wise God our Saviour, be glory and majesty, dominion and power, both now and ever" (Jude 24, 25).

From personal experience I have learned that the Christ who shed His blood for us on Calvary will never fail us.

Those who stand in the pulpit and claim that if anyone feels anxiety he or she could be possessed by a demon are insinuating that Christ has failed to protect and save that person. Flee from those people before they totally destroy your faith in God, and thus separate you from God both now and for eternity. They can never deliver you from Satan, because they have become agents of evil themselves.

To illustrate the harvest of misery produced by those who have taken upon themselves the responsibility and work of the Holy Spirit in casting out demons, I recount the experience of a woman in her 30s who had her faith in Christ's power to save totally destroyed. The following excerpts are from a very long letter.

"My husband and I," she wrote, "joined the SDA church in the fall of 1987, and observing the Sabbath was a most delightful experience. Belonging to God's commandment-keeping people was most rewarding, and I can honestly say that our joy in the Lord was perfect.

"Like many other individuals, I have been anxious about many things. I worried about the children if they were late getting home from school and was uneasy about my mother's health. At times I feared that my husband may have had an accident when he did not get home at the usual time.

"I have always been tense while riding in someone else's car. Electrical storms frightened me greatly, and a number of other things caused me concern in my life.

"Then one day as I listened to a sermon by a minister active in conducting exorcisms, I was amazed to hear how many demon-possessed Christians had the same anxieties that I experienced. The more I listened, the more I became convinced that I was also demon-possessed.

"The preacher was so convincing. Because he appeared to be such a man of God, I didn't question anything he said. And it greatly distressed me when I thought that Jesus in whom I had placed all my trust had not been able to keep demonic spirits from possessing my body. Devastated, I agreed to go through a deliverance service as a means of getting rid of the evil spirits.

"The service lasted many hours, and as the demons came up, the minister took authority over each one of them. The spirits told how they had controlled my life—they confessed it all."

The woman states in her letter that for a short while she felt released from her anxieties. In fact, she found herself not caring much about anything, a strange reaction for her. Before long her life became a tangled mess, and at times she thought about ending it all. The experience had greatly damaged her mind.

"It's hard for me to finish anything that I have started," she comments. "My memory is fading. Things that I once could remember well, now takes such effort to recall. It disheartens me to the point that I don't care what happens to me. I feel like I want to commit myself to an insane asylum, as I can't stand the pressures of life.

"My mind is under constant attack from some unseen force. The harassment, the oppression that I have been under—no one can understand. I feel like the Lord has turned away from me, and I am powerless to do anything about it. I have no desire to pray, and when I try, I get nowhere.

"My husband left me two years ago, and I can't blame him for it. I hate myself for being this screwed up. All my hopes and dreams have been dashed."

She claims that SDA ministers have not been of help to her. Not knowing what to do in her situation, they feel uncomfortable around her and avoid her. The woman closed her long letter with the plea "Mr. Morneau, I need help! I need to be at peace." How God will help her, I do not yet know. But I do know that others can escape such grief and misery by avoiding the dangers of the deliverance ministries.

Epilogue

My Second Life

Of all the comments I have received during my life, none has brought as good a feeling and appreciation for my Creator as one my cardiologist made after taking care of me for almost eight years.

Hilda and I were about to leave New York for California, and I had just completed my last checkup with him. After we finished the EKG, SMA-12, and other tests, I went into his private office. There he began commenting on some of the points in my medical case that had amazed him and his colleagues over the years. He mentioned how a battery of tests conducted in 1985 indicated that I should not have enough strength to get out of bed.

"It was exciting for me to see you walk without any indication that there was anything wrong with your heart," he said. "You are an amazing man, Roger."

The way he stared at me prompted me to reply, "You make me feel as though I had come back from the dead."

After a long pause, he replied, "You almost have, Roger; you almost have." Leaning back in his chair, he thought a moment. "I feel that you have been given a second life. Value it, Roger, and count yourself a very fortunate person."

As I drove back home, I found myself recalling Psalm 105:1-5:

"O give thanks unto the Lord; call upon
his name: make known his deeds
among the people.
"Sing unto him, sing psalms unto him;
talk ye of all his wondrous works.
"Glory ye in his holy name: let the heart
of them rejoice that seek the Lord.
"Seek the Lord, and his strength: seek
his face evermore.
"Remember his marvelous works that
he hath done; his wonders, and the
judgments of his mouth."

At this time I would like to exalt my Lord and Saviour, Jesus, by telling how He has kept me alive for the past few years.

In December 1984 as I lay dying in the intensive care unit of the Greater Niagara General Hospital in Niagara Falls, Ontario, God honored my prayers for the patients around me. Many of them became well overnight. A man whose doctor had pronounced dead suddenly revived as I pleaded for him before the Great High Priest as He ministered in the Holy of Holies of the heavenly sanctuary. According to his wife, who has kept in contact with Hilda, he lived an additional five years in perfect health.

As I saw the Spirit of God at work, and actually felt the glory of Christ's divine majesty in the place, I realized that my Lord and Saviour could break the power of death. Conversing with my Redeemer, I asked that, if it was pleasing in His sight, I would like to remain alive so I could continue to pray for others the rest of my days.

God honored my request, and a week later to the day and time I had been admitted, I walked out of that hospital under my own power. A few days after I arrived home in Endicott, New York, my cardiologist had me admitted to one of our local hospitals for an extensive series of tests. He wanted to find out the exact condition of my heart and what treatment I needed.

The tests determined that I had cardiomyopathy. A virus had done irreparable damage to my heart. A large part of the wall of the left ventricle had died. The doctor told Hilda that medical science could do nothing for me. The dead area of heart muscle would disintegrate, and when the heart could no longer pump blood, I would die. But the doctor had a big surprise coming.

Every day I asked our heavenly Father to bless my damaged heart with the power of "the Spirit of life in Christ Jesus" (Romans 8:2). I besought Him to impart to me the strength to meet the needs and demands of each day so that I might get to know Him and "the power of His resurrection" better.

Weeks, then months—eventually a year—went by. Finally the cardiologist ordered a set of tests to see what was keeping me alive. I did not learn the reason behind these tests until I moved to California. Now I can understand why every so often he would tell me that I was a walking miracle.

In April of 1992 Hilda and I moved to be with our daughter and her family in the Golden State. As soon as my medical records arrived, my new doctor did an unusual thing by asking me to come in for an appointment.

"You are a very fortunate man to be alive," he said, explaining that my heart condition in 1985 was much worse than my New York doctor had given me to understand. My heart had enlarged and, in doing so, had blocked the main artery—the aorta—by 80 percent. Another artery was 85 percent closed off, and that alone, he said, could have caused my death.

The California physician suggested a new battery of tests, including nuclear scanning and imaging of the heart. He hoped that would help him understand why I was doing as well as I was.

The new tests indicated that the blockage of the aorta had shrunk by 50 percent. The obstruction in the other artery has completely cleared. The dead part of the heart, instead of disintegrating, had turned into a hard substance. While it is inflexible, the blood supply still pumps along. The doctor agrees with me that I am kept alive only by the power of prayer.

My heart operates at 45 percent of normal capacity, which

keeps me confined to home, as I tire with every little exertion. Naturally I spend a great amount of time lying down, and I have to rest on my left side to prevent my heart from aching.

I am not unhappy about my disability—in fact, I welcome it, as it gives me the time needed to carry on my prayer ministry. Had the Lord restored me to perfect health, it would have greatly limited my time to pray for people. Everyone would have expected me to fulfill the speaking engagements that come to me from everywhere.

My rewards are many. Daily I receive letters that tell how the Lord blesses people. The power of the Spirit of God is transforming lives and resolving hopeless situations. Those letters and telephone calls bring a joy to my heart born of heaven. Like the apostle Paul, I can declare, "Most gladly therefore will I glory in my infirmities, that the power of Christ may rest upon me" (2 Corinthians 12:9).

To have been given an extended life in these closing times of earth's history is truly a wonderful gift. And to carry on a prayer ministry at the very time the Holy Spirit is making His last invitation to the human race to prepare for Christ's soon coming is indeed awesome. I can't help proclaiming, "*Glory to God in the highest*!"